Crystals
and
Numerology

Decode Your Numbers and
Support Your Life Path
with Healing Stones

EDITHA WUEST
SABINE SCHIEFERLE

EARTHDANCER

AN INNER TRADITIONS IMPRINT

First edition 2021
Crystals and Numerology
Decode Your Numbers and Support Your Life Path with Healing Stones
Editha Wuest, Sabine Schieferle

This English edition © 2021 Earthdancer GmbH
English translation © 2020 JMS books LLP
Editing by JMS books LLP (www.jmseditorial.com)

Originally published in German as: *Zahl und Stein, Heilsteine und Numerologie*
World © 2012, Neue Erde GmbH, Saarbruecken, Germany

Cover design: DesignIsIdentity.com
Crystals: Ines Blersch
Background (galaxy): Christianto/shutterstock.com
Typesetting and layout: DesignIsIdentity.com
Typeset in Sabon

Printed and bound in China by Reliance Printing Co., Ltd.

ISBN 978-1-64411-273-1 (print)
ISBN 978-1-64411-274-8 (ebook)

Published by Earthdancer, an imprint of Inner Traditions
www.earthdancerbooks.com, www.innertraditions.com

*There are moments in which every
hidden gemstone is open to the soul.*

ROBERT MUSIL
(AUSTRIAN AUTHOR)

Contents

Each chapter features the following sections:
Symbolism
Talents and Abilities
Weaknesses
Ambitions
Affirmations
Healing effects on the body

APPENDIX

*It is only when a mind is completely free that there is
the possibility of absolute deep silence;
and it is only that quality of stillness, that absolute
silence of the mind that can see that which is eternal.
This is meditation.*
KRISHNAMURTI (INDIAN AUTHOR AND TEACHER)

Introduction

This book brings together the alternative practices of numerology and crystal healing. Numerology is the study of the numerical value attributed to the letters in names and words, which helps us to build up a personal, three-dimensional character sketch, through which we can learn a great deal about our strengths, weaknesses, and life path.

Combining crystals with numbers derived from certain letters activates archetypal forces within us, exerting an influence on the subtle energy system that is housed within every human being.

Each number and letter, each crystal, person, and animal, indeed everything that is visible upon this Earth, is born of divine concepts that create vibrations via colors and sounds, and thereby radiate energies.

I (Editha Wuest) have been working with healing crystals for more than ten years. I also use them to help with my numerological consultations. These natural treasures not only help to balance out the weaknesses of a number that has been calculated for a person, but also provide support for their strengths.

After a short introduction to numerology and crystal healing, this book examines the numbers from 0 to 9 and the healing crystals associated with each.

Very best wishes,
Editha Wuest and Sabine Schieferle

Cautions Using Crystal Numerology

All the numbers you calculate and every insight you achieve should be viewed without judgment, as every number has its strengths and weaknesses. There is no good or evil, no right or wrong.

We recommend that you try out the many different effects of crystals for yourself and remain open to the inspiration that we hope to pass on in this book. Our crystal recommendations will be most effective where an individual is lacking in energy.

However, the authors and the publishers offer no guarantees and accept no liability whatsoever in respect of the contents of this book. In the event of a serious health complaint, please consult your doctor or alternative practitioner.

Numerological evaluations should only be carried out with the consent of the person to be assessed. The exceptions here are family members, deceased persons, or those who have made their data publicly available, such as politicians, actors, musicians, and so on. You should avoid passing judgment or condemning anyone.

The results of an analysis should of course not be discussed with any third parties.

All name analysis is energy work, and changes can be brought about that will also have consequences. Please bear in mind the law of cause and effect; here too, we must take responsibility for our actions, even if our aim is simply to help someone.

Introduction to the World of Numerology

Numerology is one of the oldest occult sciences and can deliver deep insights into our character, strengths, and weaknesses. All ancient cultures have their own mythology of numbers, and mathematicians of the past often described numbers as symbols of an all-embracing divine destiny, seeing them not as abstract signs but rather as representative of an individual's personality. It was long known in the ancient world that a person's name influenced their character and that specific attributes were encoded within a name's letters and syllables.

In numerology, a particular quality and energy is assigned to each number, allowing us to explore and answer the question of who we are in depth. We simply have to ask which numbers are relevant to us and which are not; the numbers will reveal their wisdom. We can decode our destinies from our names and dates of birth. Numerology expands horizons and allows us to view and understand life from different perspectives. It reveals the talents and inclinations inherent in us at the hour of our birth, and it can also help us to take a holistic view of any rebirth or new beginning in life, including marriage, founding a business, joining a company, or buying a house. Everything that bears a name can be evaluated in numbers and so be investigated and explained. Numerology involves the calculating and interpreting of these numbers. So, in summary, numerological calculations can teach us more about:

- our names, our dates of birth, and our characters
- our abilities and talents, our missions and aims in life
- our strengths and weaknesses
- our ideal profession
- new perspectives in our lives
- the ideal time for change

In numerology we can analyze our own (or someone else's) name by calculating our expression number (sometimes known as our "destiny number"), our heart's desire number, and our personality number, as well as our realization number and soul motivation (calculated by adding up the digits derived from the initial letters of our name).

This book investigates our expression number, life path number, and realization number. Our **expression number** (**EN**) reveals our earthly karma and bears our destiny and the character we receive from our family. It encompasses our personality and the manner in which we master our life path.

Our **life path number** (**LPN**) reveals our destiny and our individual purpose on Earth, as well as the talents and abilities that we should develop or discard.

Our **realization number** (**RN**) is particularly indicative of what is and/or will be of importance in the second half of our life (from our 34th birthday onward, in other words, from our 35th year) and our potential to act positively. Our subconscious comprehends what is still important in life, what is yet be done, and what is still to be learned. It is then that we will recognize and harvest the "fruits of our labors," reap our rewards.

Finding Our Personal Numbers

We calculate the numbers listed below from our names and dates of birth. (See *Calculating the Numbers*, page 15.) The numbers for name analysis change when we marry, as the vibrations of the new family are taken into account.

Our earthly karma gives us our:

- expression number
- heart's desire number
- personality number
- destiny path number
- soul motivation

Our **realization number** (**RN**) is created from the link between our earthly and cosmic karma. Our cosmic karma governs the following:

- life path number
- birth day number

Our **expression number** (EN) is calculated by adding together the numerical values (numbers 1–9) attributed to each letter in our birth name (using our first and last names).

It shows our earthly karma and carries our destiny and the character we receive from our family. It reveals our personality and the way we will master our life journey.

Our **heart's desire number** (HDN) is calculated by adding together the numerical values attributed to each vowel in our birth name (first and last names).

It reveals our personality, our innermost emotions, and our feelings toward other people and our environment.

Our **personality number** (PN) is calculated by adding together the numerical values attributed to each consonant in our birth name (first and last names).

This number reveals the impression we make on the outside world, how others see us, and what they expect of us, based on their impression and image of us.

Our **life path number** (LPN) is calculated by adding together the single-digit numbers in our date of birth.

This number reveals our destiny and purpose on Earth, along with the talents and abilities we should develop or accept.

(See the sample calculation derived from a date in *Calculating the Numbers*, page 19.)

Our **birth day number** (**BDN**) is calculated using the number(s) of the day of our birth. For example, for someone born 7 June, their BDN is 7; for someone born 21 June, their BDN is 2 + 1 = 3.

It shows our past, our mental and spiritual legacy, and the essence of our last life. We should recognize this as a gift to be used for positive ends. We can use it to obtain important additional information about our life path number.

Our **destiny path number** (**DPN**) is calculated by adding together the single-digit heart's desire and personality numbers. It is identical with our expression number.

Our destiny path number shows us the path we should find and follow.

Our **realization number** (**RN**) is calculated by adding together our single-digit expression and life path numbers.

This number is particularly indicative of what is and/or will be of importance in the second half of our lives (from our 34th birthday), in addition to our potential for action and the results we will achieve.

Our **soul motivation number** (**SM**) is calculated by adding together the numbers derived from the initial letters of our name.

This number reveals why we are on this Earth, what we want to learn, and what we should learn. In a way, our soul motivation opens the door to our destiny path.

Which personal numbers do I bring to the table?

We receive our names from our parents and, since we have all been born, we all have a date of birth. These numbers have much to say about our path, our aim in life, and the obstacles we must overcome. Knowledge of our personal numbers will make us aware of our obligations and the options for change that we can expect in our lives.

Through the names we receive from our clan—our family—we bring our *earthly karma and our "free will."* It is through free will that the divine allows us to live in freedom. We receive our genes for our lives here on Earth from our parents, while we "receive" impressions, sets of beliefs, emotions, experiences, and traditions, both for good and for ill, from our wider family.

Numerology reveals our abilities and weaknesses, with the latter enabling us to see which issues require attention or need to be "worked on" in order to return things to an even keel. Our earthly karma encompasses teachings and instructions for certain ways to behave, but also warnings, and there is a good reason for this. We are here to learn and to constantly develop ourselves spiritually; the pointers we receive are signposts that indicate the path we should follow toward the fulfillment of our cosmic karma.

We receive our *cosmic karma, our "divine will,"* on our birth-DAY. This divine will leads us to our life purpose and helps us to fulfill our spiritual mission. The growth required to achieve this through our spiritual awareness is encoded in our date of birth.

It is settled in a sort of contract in the spiritual world before our actual birth and so we are born on a particular day and at a very particular hour.

Our name encompasses our earthly karma, the free will to shape our life.

The genes we receive from our families contribute:
- impressions (left by experiences)
- emotions
- health
- experiences
- traditions

Our date of birth encompasses our cosmic karma, our ability to perceive divine will. What experiences does the soul need to undergo? What do we have to learn in this life? What path have we embarked upon?

Calculating the Numbers

We are equipped with our personal life path and expression numbers from the very start of our lives; they provide information about the lessons we will have to learn and the spiritual growth and personal development of which we are capable. Many people have similar or even identical numbers, our "number buddies," but due to our individual life circumstances each of us leads our life and numbers differently from our number buddies. A person's culture and environment also influence their path in life, while their inherited genes and impressions also shape them. Our interests, convictions, and values make us all very individual people, but at some point, certain questions always crop up: Who am I? Where do I come from? Where is my path taking me?

A good way to embark upon answering these questions is to analyze your name. Were you aware of just how great an influence your name has? A person's name is never chosen by chance; it corresponds to the soul's mission, concerns, and interests. Our name helps us to fulfill our mission in life.

In this chapter, we show *how* these calculations are made, using the numbers 0 to 9 and the double and/or master numbers 11, 22, 33 and 44.

Using the table on page 18, a numerical value (a vibration) can be assigned to each letter. Write the corresponding numerical values under the letters of the word or name that you wish to calculate; all the numbers are then added up and reduced down to a single-digit number. For example, if the total comes to 26, add these numbers together to produce the single-digit number 8.

Sample name calculation

Each name has a very particular characteristic vibration. Each letter is assigned to a number, and each number has its own meaning. This meaning or connotation gives each name its individual energy and makes a resonant connection with our fellow human beings.

Use your first name and family name, as printed in your passport, for the name calculation. We identify with these names as they currently have the strongest vibration (this is especially true for men and women who have taken the name of their partner).

An individual's maiden name always remains a central aspect of them, with an important basic message. It is always interesting to calculate using a person's maiden name to see which life topics were of significance before marriage.

Additional elements of a name (such as di, de, or of, as in "duke of") are included in the calculation, as are titles such as Professor or Doctor in their shortened form (Prof., Dr., and so on). Names from other languages or cultures should be calculated in their original form and/or language, although the vibration of the letters and numbers will have the same significance.

Hyphenated first names and double names are viewed as one name, so Anne-Marie becomes AnneMarie and Armstrong-Jones becomes ArmstrongJones. Additional forenames (or their initial letters) that are used regularly should also be included in the calculation. If the expression number that is arrived at does not harmonize very well with a life path number, additional forenames or abbreviations can be included in the calculation. An example of a simple calculation is provided overleaf.

Sample expression number calculation

Replace the letters with the numbers, using the Pythagorean conversion table below.

1	2	3	4	5	6	7	8	9
A	B	C	D	E	F	G	H	I
J	K	L	M	N	O	P	Q	R
S	T	U	V	W	X	Y	Z	

The more often you work with the table, the easier it is to use.

J	A	N	E	D	O	E
1	1	5	5	4	6	5

Add together the digits in the row of numbers above.

In this case, the number is 27, which is then reduced to a single-digit number.

Step 1: $1 + 1 + 5 + 5 + 4 + 6 + 5 = 27$
Step 2: $2 + 7 = 9$

Jane Doe's expression number is therefore 9.

Judging yourself is difficult, and it is important to be objective and follow your intuition. Be honest when examining your weaknesses; accept them but make sure you forge a connection to your strengths. Every number has positive and negative vibrations. We must be aware of which side we are on at any given moment.

Sample life path number calculation

A birth year is written in full: **1975** (not just 75).

> Let's take the date of birth 9/16/1975 as an example, and calculate as follows:
> = 9 + 1 + 6 + 1 + 9 + 7 + 5 = 38
> = 3 + 8 = 11

Jane Doe's life path number is therefore 11.

First, add up the individual digits in the date of birth to produce a subtotal. Then add up the digits in this subtotal until arriving at a single-digit number or a master number. In the example shown above, we arrive at a double number, 11 (see *Double and Master Numbers*, page 21). As it is a double (and a master) number, we do not add up the digits again to reduce them to a single-digit number.

Sample realization number calculation

Once you have worked out your expression and life path numbers, add these two single-digit numbers together to calculate your realization number. The realization number shows what is and/or will be important in the second half of our lives (from our 34th birthday onward). It reveals what influence or impact we may have, what we are striving for deep in our hearts, and the rewards that we can achieve as a result of our efforts.

$$9 + 11 = 20$$
$$2 + 0 = 2$$

The realization number is 2.

You now know how to calculate the number for any name, word, or date. Over the following pages, we explain how to find our personal numbers and then to explain their meaning. Some may come as a surprise, others will be confirmed, and some will still need to be identified, developed, and implemented. Applying our understanding of numbers in a practical way involves living out the positive characteristics in our life while being aware of the negative. By focusing on our life path, with all our thoughts and desires, we nourish its development. And the more often we use the power of thought to find a solution for the tasks in hand, the closer we will get to our goal.

Important: always check and double-check your numbers using the chart. Mistakes are easily made.

Double and Master Numbers

Double and master numbers are created when a double digit occurs in an expression number, a date of birth, or a realization number: for example, the number 1 in 29/11, 38/11, or 47/11, or the double digits in 22, 33, and 44.

Double numbers, also known as higher numbers, have the same significance as single-digit numbers but represent a considerable amplification of the potential. The numbers 11, 22, 33, and 44 are the principal higher numbers and should not be reduced to a single-digit base number for symbolic reasons—the numbers 1, 2, and 3 are spiritual numbers, and we create matter with the number 4. The double numbers 55, 66, 77, 88, and 99 are subordinated vibrations of the 4 higher numbers.

Double numbers offer an opportunity to overcome obstacles and difficulties in life and to pass tests.

Our progress in life is constantly being "tested" by certain situations or hurdles that we must overcome, which reinforces the experiences we have had so far. These tests become increasingly smaller and therefore less problematic with time, until we have finally mastered the lessons that need learning. When the negative aspects of the double numbers have been worked through and only positive aspects remain in our life, the double numbers become master numbers.

Higher numbers require a great deal of energetic work, but also offer great opportunities for success.

Master numbers are similarly double combinations of the numbers 1, 2, 3 and 4 (11, 22, 33, and 44, for example), but also these same numbers repeated three or four times (111, 2222, 333, 4444, and so on). This doubling represents an amplification of the base number, with the positive aspects of the numbers being expressed in a boosted form in the master numbers. The task here is to reconcile opposites—exterior and interior, body and mind, head and heart.

Double numbers work on an earth-bound, material plane while master numbers involve potential on a spiritual level. People with a master number are tested by destiny until the particular number's learning goal has been reached. This means that the energies of these master numbers are blocked until the positive aspects become part of an individual's life. People can become role models and advisors for their fellow humans through their experiences and learning processes.

Through the doubling of its influence, the vibration of the single number will become so clear that in its final form it is masterful. We are connected to our higher selves; we integrate divine knowledge into our lives, increasing the total vibration. This spiritual illumination is completely integrated into our subtle bodies. We melt into the realm of our soul, as it were, and become masters of our lives.

This mastery involves a lengthy process of development, experience, and insight, requiring significant energetic work on a physical, mental, and spiritual level. Make your double and/or master number your favorite number; you will come across it frequently in your daily life and it will confirm that you are on the right path.

What Do Numbers and Healing Crystals Have in Common?

All cosmic existence is united within collective principles and laws; shared properties and qualities are reflected in different people, animals, plants, crystals, symbols, and objects, and are expressed in the widest range of forms and sounds. People (for example) can come into resonance with this shared vibration using certain crystals, just as numerological symbolism resonates with healing crystals.

The assigning of numbers to particular crystals is therefore based on their common factors; they express the same qualities on different planes of being. Numbers are highly complex and several crystals can be assigned to them, as we explain in the pages that follow. For this book we have selected those crystals that we consider are best suited to the particular numbers and will be of particular help to users as they reinforce their talents and abilities and express their respective goals. Where weaknesses of character or negative impressions are present, crystals similarly have a strong balancing influence, and at times it can be quite a challenge to choose healing crystals for numbers that do not feature in a calculation.

Our selection should not be seen as being totally set in stone; instead, it should be used as a prompt to try out a wide range of crystals to discover which healing crystal raises your energy and provides support in a particular situation. We would encourage everyone to be open to discovering the many effects of healing crystals.

Crystals can be selected according to their effects, but also by using kinesiological tests, a biotensor (a measuring and testing device) or pendulum, or even by color.

Introduction to
the World of Healing Crystals

How Do Healing Crystals Work?

Healing crystals carry an eternity within them. They are Mother Earth's treasures; their beauty, luster, color, and clarity fascinate us. However, healing crystals are not simply esthetic, they also possess healing powers. They promote our development and guide us toward physical health and spiritual well-being.

Today, with our pills, treatments, and ointments, we could be forgiven for wondering what on earth crystals might be able to do for us. How can a crystal, clearly an inert stone, exert an influence on a living organism? The answer is that it does so through the vibration of its natural colors and crystalline structures, its chemical components, its density, and its hardness. In addition, healing crystals connect us with the strengthening vibrations of Mother Earth while simultaneously passing on cosmic energies.

Every crystal contains within it a divine primary principle, an archetypal structure, and a basic concept, and it is with this basic concept, this cosmic vibration, that we resonate when we make contact with a crystal. Since everything in life is based on vibrations and vital energy reacts most powerfully to the subtlest of stimuli, these energies can restore balance to our vitality.

Combining healing crystals with numbers allows us to get our fleeting and all-too-human negative emotions under control, such as anger, envy, rage, resentment, arrogance, deceitfulness, greed, jealousy, or insecurity. The ultimate goal is self-knowledge, a stable character, and balanced personal development, protecting us from mental and psychosomatic illness. People who use crystals are open to healing, since the crystal passes on information to the person carrying it while also activating certain energy centers (chakras and meridians) and cleansing (and also stabilizing) the aura.

Many people feel an immediate effect when wearing or carrying a crystal; some experience a sense of physical warmth or relaxation, feelings of joy and love, or a release of negative thought patterns.

Modern crystal healing makes it possible for many people to access knowledge of the effects of gemstones. When we wear a crystal or place it on our bodies, universal forces and structures are released, capable of healing blockages, tension, and illnesses on a physical level.

Many of our own experiences and those reported by other users, along with crystal healing handbooks, confirm the specific and special ways in which healing crystals work.

Using Healing Crystals Correctly

When we resonate with healing crystals, they take in vibrations from our negative thoughts and feelings and pass on their own positive energy to those wearing them. In this way they cleanse and protect, although they may also lose their strength, change in color, or even emit undesirable energies. This is why it is important to purify these precious stones from time to time. When working with a new crystal, it can be cleansed before use—freed from external vibrations (arising from processing, storage, and so on)—as follows:

- Hold the crystal under running water and in your mind picture negative aspects being carried away by the water. The crystal can also be placed on a piece of amethyst druse. Amethyst is the only crystal that remains neutral, transforming all impurities.

    If a crystal has been previously used in healing therapy, it is a good idea to immerse it in a weak solution of sea salt and water. Do note, however, that not all crystals are suitable for this cleansing treatment in which the crystal comes into direct contact with the salt solution (such as turquoise, malachite, azurite, selenite, among others). If in doubt, place the crystal in a small glass bowl, then place the bowl in the salt solution.

- After each cleansing, recharge the crystal's energy by placing it in a glass bowl or a wide flat dish in daylight (but not in direct sunlight). Crystals can also be cleansed and recharged with the power of thought or imagination.

    Use your intuition to tell when the crystal is completely pure and reenergized once more.

If crystals are made to work too hard, they can become dull and unappealing or even develop cracks. If a crystal should fall on a hard surface and break in two, it will not be by chance, it will probably have absorbed significant negative vibrations from the wearer. In which case, the wearer should thank the crystal for its help and return it to Mother Earth.

Treat crystals with love and care, and store them in a peaceful, pleasant place. Connect with them as often as possible and they will be true companions at your side.

Using healing crystals: A chosen crystal can be worn on a ribbon or chain, as a bracelet or in another piece of jewelry. They can also be attached to a specific part of the body with a hypoallergenic bandage, either where pain is felt or over a particular organ that needs to be stimulated or soothed. Crystals can be carried about with you during the day, for example in a pocket. They can also be placed on chakras, held in the hand at night as you fall asleep, or placed under a pillow.

Healing crystals will bring positive, balancing energies to living areas or the workplace positioned beside a computer or placed on a desk. The harmonic vibrations of an amethyst druse help you to relax.

The energies of healing crystals can also be absorbed by drinking crystal water. Place a small crystal among your cosmetics or toiletries and the crystal vibrations will be transmitted to the skin and influence your aura.

Every color has a particular emotive impact that differs
from that of other colors.
JOLANDE JACOBI (AUSTRIAN PSYCHOLOGIST)

Nature, all around us, is full of color. Colors are vibrations, part of light, and they give us the gift of energy for life. We use color in expressions to describe ourselves every day: "red in the face with anger," "blue with cold," or "green with envy." Although we cannot actually see our mental health in the way we can see our bodily health, our mental condition can nevertheless have noticeable effects on us physically. It therefore follows that colors can affect us, too, as we know from color theory and from color and crystal therapy. Even ancient civilizations such as the Egyptians, Incas, and Mayans used healing practices involving color. Each color has its own vibrational frequency that resonates with our physical, mental, and spiritual vibrations.

Just like healing crystals, color can be a vital force and source of strength if used correctly. Each color makes certain physical vibrational frequencies visible and so can have a positive or negative effect on our well-being. Color can influence certain of our organs and nerves and stimulate the growth of cells within the body.

We can draw conclusions about life situations, moods, and even physical conditions from a liking for or disliking of a particular color. We should ask ourselves why we are not keen on red, for example, or loathe the color purple. Do we find choosing the color of clothes or deciding which healing crystal to select a challenge?

Healing crystals and their colors bring us into contact with extremely subtle energetic vibrations that help us to achieve harmony and balance.

Red is the color of vitality, emotionality, and assertiveness. It has an exciting, warming, and stimulating effect. It makes people talkative, willing to work, impulsive, and self-confident. This color helps us to set new goals, reinforces our powers of perseverance, and promotes courage, decisiveness, purposefulness, dynamism, strength, and steadfastness.

Orange has the strongest signal effect and is the color of joy, creative expression, impulsiveness, and self-confidence. Orange also has a cheering, relaxing, and calming effect. This color elicits self-possession, independence, self-assurance, sociability, and cheerfulness. It is the most active and energetic shade, encouraging expansiveness and even extrovert behavior. Orange helps us to combat depression, melancholy, discontent, and world weariness.

Yellow is the color of enlightenment, wisdom, thinking, inner freedom, and liberty. Yellow stimulates the mind and helps with memory lapses and learning difficulties. It promotes logical thinking, self-awareness, merriment, optimism, and a zest for life. Yellow counteracts weariness, dark moods, and listlessness.

Green is the color of inner harmony and balance, plenty, growth, and a healthy existence. Green promotes regeneration, relaxation, and equalization. It has a calming, healing, and rejuvenating effect. This color reinforces empathy, security, reliability, and imagination, stimulating mental images.

Blue is the color of the spirit and belief, peace and calm, devotion, truth, and loyalty. It represents the unconscious, inner silence, and mental depth. Blue promotes honesty, recognition, and the search for truth. It soothes, harmonizes, and brings relaxation and balance. This bolsters our patience, loyalty, sincerity, and confidence.

Indigo is the color of spiritual internalization and the extrasensory perception of hidden mysteries. Indigo promotes states of higher consciousness and extrasensory awareness. It brings the gift of idealism and encourages social activities. This color represents health in mind, body, and spirit.

Violet is the color of transformation, of alchemy, magic, and mysticism. Violet represents spiritual experiences and supports our intuition, while promoting perception and concentration. It serves to expand our consciousness, brings inspiration, and encourages love of our neighbor, idealism, and selflessness.

Brown is the color of Mother Earth. It represents consistency, stability, persistence, and perseverance. This color encourages practical, grounded, down-to-earth thinking. With brown we will not stand out from the crowd.

Black is the color of darkness, a negating of stimulation by light or color of any kind. It provides protection and security, absorbs excess energy, and helps with extreme exhaustion. It also represents the unknown, that which is yet to be. Black helps individuals to find themselves and lead them to their own light source.

White is the color of light, the mind, innocence, purity, and new beginnings. It stands for redemption, protection, and liberation from all influences; it reflects and strengthens that which already exists. White promotes an individual's ability to overcome problems and resolve conflicts.

Clear quartz and clear crystals represent clarity, purity, and perfection; they also open us up to divine consciousness. They encourage neutrality and self-knowledge.

Colored crystals provide a link with the diversity of life and unite the ways in which the colors that are present work. They bring fun and joy into life, inspire new ideas, and help us to organize our daily life without problem.

How This Book Works

Numbers reveal the strengths and weaknesses with which our personality expresses itself in this life. They deliver information.

The vibrations of **crystals** can stimulate spiritual growth and promote personal development. Our intuition—our inner voice—will develop with regular use, so that we can "hear" and understand inner messages.

I would like to present a range of different ways in which numbers can be combined with healing crystals:

First, calculate your expression number. This reveals your destiny and the character you have inherited from your family; your parents shaped you through their genes, emotions, and impressions.

If your expression number is 1, for example, begin by referring to the *Symbolism* paragraph for number 1 (see page 38). It is the ancient, divine primal force. If you would like to concentrate on the vibration of the sun, the neutral, male aspect of life, I would recommend the ruby. Your extended family and your parents, who chose you, gave you great strength and energy for your path in life. You will be a pioneer, forging your way ahead, and can call the positive talents and abilities of number 1 your own.

If you feel you lack some of number 1's positive qualities, look at the relevant crystals to see if they can encourage these qualities.

To target a specific problem, look at your number's "weaknesses" and try working with the crystals associated with these. Don't force anything, however; the right moment to receive healing and the answers to life's questions will come.

Now calculate your life path number. It reveals your vocation and the main challenges for you in this incarnation, along with everything that your soul consciousness wishes to learn. If your life path number is 5, for example, as with your expression number, refer to the section on number 5 and read it through to the end, noting what speaks to you the most and what should be learned or transformed, and find a suitable crystal to do this.

Follow the same procedure to identify your realization number.

Having found your three most important crystals, you can now begin to work with them.

Crystals can be applied to the body. You can wear them as jewelry; for example, take three drilled tumbled stones (standing for each of your EN, LPN, and RN numbers) and thread them onto a ribbon to make a necklace. Or buy a chain, a pendant, or a bracelet containing a crystal associated with one of the numbers you have calculated, then use your intuition to attach the two other crystals as tumbled stones to your body using a hypoallergenic bandage. Alternatively, place them on the appropriate chakras and feel the energy flowing into your aura.

Healing crystal water is another alternative. Begin by purifying the three crystals (see page 27). Now take three large drinking glasses and place one of the tumbled stones or natural crystals in each. Top up the glasses with tap water, leave to stand for about 10 or 15 minutes in daylight (not direct sunlight), then drink the energized water over the course of the day. It will be especially effective if you draw the symbol of your number on several small sheets of colored paper and write a suitable affirmation beside it, then place a paper under each glass. Affirmations are positive statements whose purpose is to encourage and motivate. They say "yes" to life, helping us to transform our doubts and convert negative into positive thoughts. The water helps to absorb these additional good vibrations.

Affirmations can also be stored on an appropriate crystal. Write a positive and constructive sentence on a sheet of paper and take this in your left (transmitting) hand, while holding the crystal in your right (receiving) hand. Now imagine your left hand passing on the information to your right hand. Feel how the energy of the affirmation is passed into the crystal through your heart center. The energized crystal can now be carried with you.

Use your personal calculated numbers to make a code. Let's say your expression number is 37/1, your life path number is 23/5, and your realization number is 18/9. A short code could be made using each last single-digit number to make 159, or you could make a nine-digit code: 371 235 189.

Write your code, along with your three most important affirmations, on sheets of colored paper and arrange them around your home. Place one under your pillow or on a desk, or attach one to the bathroom mirror. Softly recite your code with its affirmations. Alternatively, store them on a healing crystal.

Once you have worked out the number for your name, you will also have a code that can bring you happiness.

Take for example the name Eve Summers (5 + 4 + 5 + 1 + 3 + 4 + 4 + 5 + 9 + 1). Your expression number would be 41/5. Visualize the talents and abilities for 5 and recite your expression number code very slowly: ...5...4...5...1...3...4...4...5...9...1. You might begin by reciting the code five times a day, increasing eventually to nine times a day. You will soon find that you begin to feel happy.

The Number 1

To a complete man belong the power of thought,
the power of will, and the power of the heart.
LUDWIG FEUERBACH (GERMAN PHILOSOPHER)

Symbolism

Number 1 embodies unity and insight; it is an expression of light and the highest creative powers, representing self-confidence, self-awareness, and "consciousness of self." Its symbol is a circle with a dot at the center, the dot being the seed that takes root in the material plane and fills it with light. This number is both one and all. It is perfect because it is indivisible. It is the beginning, middle, and end, the mother of all other numbers. The creative impulse and the collective potential of all ideas lie within it.

The **sun**, with its male aspect, is the principal planet of number 1. It is the center of our planetary system and governs Leo, the zodiac sign. Its energy represents the primal force and the source that delivers the gifts of light, strength, life, and vitality.

The healing crystal for 1

In ancient European cultures, **ruby** was the gemstone of the sun, reinforcing the planet's powers with its vibrations. They represent inner fire, vigor, and passion, bringing healing and sun-filled warmth and relief to deep-seated fears and traumas. They encourage leadership qualities and deliver focus to visions and ideals. Rubies bring momentum and dynamism to our lives, encouraging us to be fully alert and aware, capable, impulsive, and spontaneous. They strengthen our decisiveness and support willpower, assertiveness, drive, and courage. Number one people can motivate their peers with their own ideas and ambitions.

Talents and Abilities

Number one people are active and healthy, and are full of energy and ambition, boasting a positive aura, inventiveness, and marked creativity. They also possess a strong will and inner strength, and are honest, fair, and brave. Intelligent and lively, they are individualists, while also being a little idiosyncratic. Number ones have a great potential for starting anew. They love to explore the unknown. Fearless, and with the common good in mind, they set out to right wrongs.

They like to help and encourage their peers, spurring them on, while remaining at their side with helpful advice. Warmhearted, with particular empathy for the sick and helpless, they also look out for children. They are able to put their own interests on hold without abandoning them entirely. Number ones are leaders, bringing new ideas and projects to the table. They are quick off the mark, while also observing and guiding their peers with wise thoughts.

They are original thinkers and open to new ideas, with an ability to make a clear distinction between the essential and the

unimportant in order to act for the best. Their purposefulness, energy, and reliability lead them to success. The world has very high expectations of number one people, which in turn fires their ambition and they pursue their goals without hesitation.

Crystals that boost talents and abilities

Golden topaz, also known as **imperial topaz,** is also a stone of the sun. It encourages us to strive for fame and recognition and has been associated with rulers for centuries. It helps us to overcome potential limitations, expands horizons, and supports us in the search for a purpose in life. It releases reserves of energy and boosts activity.

This healing crystal brings self-assurance and encourages inspiration, autonomy, and self-fulfillment. It reinforces individuality and our confidence in our own abilities.

Rutilated quartz, or sunlight captured in stone, as it has been thought of since ancient times, brings light and love to new beginnings. It boosts our connection to higher spheres, reinforces our vitality, and releases inner blockages. It opens doors, triggering positive situations that we may never previously have considered possible. Stimulating our spiritual growth and energy flow, it also supports us in maintaining an upright posture. This healing crystal helps us to see the bigger picture and is with us when we need to cast aside habitual behaviors that are detrimental for us and embark upon new paths, and learn to understand life from a fresh perspective.

Weaknesses

The number 1 exposes us to constant change. Number one people always look after number one! They can be selfish, tactless, domineering, intolerant, insistent, and absolutely sure of themselves, their ground, and their opinions. They incline toward egocentricity, pride, aggression, intolerance, and headstrong attitudes. Number ones are often biased, stick stubbornly to their guns, brook no contradiction, and refuse advice or criticism. They have a tendency to use other people and will try to achieve their goals by any means at their disposal. When they find someone willing to take care of things on their behalf, they may become lazy and impatient. Number one people find it difficult to accept imperfections in themselves and in others; they are perfectionists and want to control everything in their immediate environment. Showing their feelings or offering forgiveness does not come easy to them.

Crystals that balance out weaknesses

Citrine* is a wonderful crystal with considerable power and energy. It supports a sunny disposition and delivers well-being and vitality. This healing crystal brings self-assurance and confidence and instills a sense of self-fulfillment. It also promotes individuality, harmony, and a zest for life.

Citrine refreshes brain cells and monitors our nervous system. It helps us to process and deal with experiences and insights,

---

* Please ensure that you buy citrine that has not been burned or heat-treated.

allowing us to shut the door on the past. This gemstone is our companion when we face resistance: no obstacle is too big, no road too long! It helps us to realize our ideas, goals, desires, and ambitions with serenity and confidence in times of stress.

Sunstone gives us the strength to change things and is consistently useful for helping us to recharge our batteries. It brings the gifts of optimism and drive, alleviates depression, and transforms fears and worries.

Ambitions

Number one people aim to go through life with self-confidence and self-awareness. They want to stand up for what they believe in and find success in love. They strive for perfection in all aspects of life.

Number ones are role models and pioneers. They seek to discover and explore new horizons; they enjoy introducing fresh ideas and positive thoughts into the world. Their individuality, willpower, and intellect help them in this respect. Each challenge strengthens them a little more and they find it advantageous to trust their own feelings. However, they should also listen to the opinions of others in order to broaden their perspectives. The more number ones learn to communicate with their peers on the same level and to respect them as such, the greater their true qualities and personal impact will be. They will then be astute leaders capable of bringing out the potential of others. It is only by being without prejudice and judgment that they will become truly aware and able to live life without wanting to control it or to predict the future. Their courage, strength, and mental capacity can inspire others.

Crystals that support ambitions

Clear quartz brings light. It reinforces our aura, provides protection, and combats negative energies. Its unwavering radiance contains all the colors of the rainbow. It connects us with the divine light that dwells within the depths of our souls and illuminates our deepest being.

It delivers the gifts of strength and courage, bringing structure and order to our thoughts. It releases aura blockages and impurities and soothes discord. Clear quartz has a harmonizing effect, helping us to remain neutral and introducing calm into our lives as it balances our energies. It promotes development, intuition, and self-knowledge. It opens us up to divine inspiration and connects us with the universal power of the Creator.

Natural diamond* is a genuinely masterful healer and a very intense crystal. Its vibrations serve the talents of number ones and activate harmony with their "higher self."

"Learn to recognize and accept your shadows and bring your light to shine within, and then you will be an enlightened being."

Affirmations

- I am courageous; full of power, I shall conquer the world.
- I am active and attract success and everything I could possibly need.
- I perfectly express my divine light.

---

*Natural diamonds are generally bought as part of a chain or pendant, but their effects are also valued in the form of diamond water.

Amber is also the stone, or light, of the sun. It supports us when we put our plans into practice and assists us in completing tasks successfully.

It is a helpful companion in daily life, making us carefree and cheerful.

Garnet reinforces our courage and willpower, sparking joy in our activities and helping us to see things through.

Tiger's eye helps us to look within ourselves and identify those things that will do us good.

Healing effects on the body

Ruby strengthens the heart and blood circulation, helps to fight off infectious diseases and inflammation, and is also used to treat ear conditions. It can help to lower cholesterol levels and to ease varicose veins and chronic tiredness.

Golden topaz stimulates the whole body, including the taste buds. It reinforces the spine and heart, eases asthma attacks, and provides support against arteriosclerosis (hardening of the arteries) and digestive conditions.

Rutilated quartz alleviates asthma, bronchitis, and heart pain, eases tightness in the chest area, strengthens the skin, and supports an upright posture.

Citrine cleanses and detoxifies the bowels, strengthens the nerves, and helps with diabetes, bloating, stomach cramps, and circulatory disorders. It is also effective for weather sensitivity, erectile dysfunction, bed-wetting, and multiple sclerosis.

Sunstone boosts the heart, has a healing effect on circulatory disorders, and stimulates the autonomic nervous system.

Clear quartz has a wide spectrum of healing powers. It eases conditions that include dizziness, balance problems, nausea, and diarrhea. It has a cooling effect on burns and sunburn, and it also helps with eye conditions and thyroid problems.

Natural diamond supports the body's cleansing processes. It is very good after a stroke. It strengthens the kidneys and bladder, improves hypothyroidism, and combats the aging process.

Amber promotes the self-healing process, warms the body, eases the symptoms of influenza, asthma, and psoriasis, and is effective in ear, nose, and throat complaints. It maintains balance with the endocrine glands and liver function, and it can also relieve teething pain in infants.

Garnet supports the production of blood. It alleviates rheumatism, arthritis, skin complaints, and calcification.

Tiger's eye strengthens the bones and joints, eases inflammation of the knee joints, helps fight colds, warms the body, and sharpens eyesight. It is recommended for those giving up smoking and in particular those undergoing cancer therapy.

The Number 2

To realize our dreams, we must decide to wake up.
JOSEPHINE BAKER (FRANCO-AMERICAN DANCER)

Symbolism

Number 2 is symbolized by two semicircles. It represents duality and polar opposites—Heaven and Earth, good and evil, positive and negative. This reciprocity expresses the inseparable and dynamic connection of all life. The principal planet for number two people is the moon, which governs the zodiac sign Cancer. The moon is linked to the rhythms of life and the cycles of the Earth and the human body. It is expressed in particular in femininity and the circle of fertility, conception, birth, and motherhood. Similarly, it also reflects our shadow sides, the unconscious, the dark night.

The healing crystal for 2

As the name suggests, the **moonstone***is associated with the moon. It is a symbol of femininity and harmonizes the natural rhythms and cycles of a woman's body. It supports empathy and the ability to recognize feelings and moods. Both women and men can

---

* Don't confuse moonstone with white labradorite.

use moonstone to open themselves up more effectively to their inner feminine aspects. This healing crystal stimulates dreams and promotes intuition, mediumship, and extrasensory perception. It encourages gentleness and softness and brings about happy coincidences.

Talents and Abilities

Two is the number of discernment, polarity, and separation from unity; it represents yin, the feminine principle.

Number two people are calm, sensitive, considerate, empathetic, and attentive. Feelings are important for them. They are generally diplomatic, agreeable, and friendly. They are good at dealing with people and enjoy wide circles of friends and great empathy. They are adaptable, modest, companionable, passionate, and easily enthused. Number two people make gentle and loving partners. They do not like to live alone and need a sensitive partner in order to be whole and complete. They look for harmony and hope for a positive, lasting relationship.

Rose quartz emphasizes gentleness and tenderness. It brings out our desires and our caring side, making us kind and sensitive, healing emotional wounds and bringing luck in love. It frees us from worries, promotes trust, and helps us to love ourselves and to accept our fellow humans as they are. With rose quartz, we can follow our life path in light and love, gently and yet purposefully. It protects everything that is helpless and pure, and so is also suitable for babies and toddlers.

Aventurine promotes mental recovery, helping us to relax and feel good. Calming our thoughts and sensory reactions, it helps us to find rest and access our inner strength.

With aventurine we become content, more stable, and better equipped to handle pressure and can get on with making our dreams in life come true. Aventurine is known as the healing crystal "doctor," cleansing the aura and exerting a calming influence during times of stress and inner turmoil.

Weaknesses

Number two people are compliant and volatile, yet can be rather slow and cautious or even apathetic.

Moody and sensitive, they react with emotion, in particular in matters of love and friendship. They often seem restless and discontent with their lives, striving for perfection and equilibrium in all situations. At times fearful and unwilling to face difficulties, they may look the other way when conflict is in the wings. They are strongly skeptical and often hesitate, finding it difficult to make decisions and implement their ideas. They prefer to adapt to the needs of others rather than follow their own path and fulfill their own desires.

Number two people try to avoid hurting the feelings of their fellow human beings, with the result that they may appear shy or suppress their own emotions.

They prefer to wait until things resolve themselves on their own, which is rarely the case. There is a high risk of dependence with number two people, whether upon traditions or material things, or upon other people. As their inner strength is often weak, situations can be "swept under the carpet" or covered up (especially behind the haze of alcohol).

Carnelian establishes a connection with Mother Earth. It helps us to accept and overcome difficulties. It resolves karmic entanglements and helps us to let go of the past and begin to live in the present. It provides stability and eases powerful mood swings.

Carnelian supports us in problem-solving and completing tasks. It transmits warmth and gentleness and is the healing crystal of choice for creativity.

Petrified wood grounds us, supporting a down-to-earth attitude and a sense of reality, while also stabilizing our health. It helps us to keep both feet on the ground, which is very important for number two people, who with "their heads in the clouds" can fail to put their ideas into practice. Petrified wood stimulates the imagination and brings a sense of balance to thoughts and feelings.

Prehnite encourages people to open up, while discouraging avoidance and repression, allowing us to give our own identity due emphasis. It penetrates deep levels of our consciousness, making us aware of suppressed events and memories and enabling us to perceive negative vibrations.

Ambitions

Number 2 prompts us to develop and use our sensitivity, intuition, and psychic abilities. The goal of number two people is to find deep insights and inner peace, as well as to be centered and stable in life.

When they let go of their doubts, fears, and indecision, they open themselves up to the new in all aspects of life. They should learn to distinguish between the important and the unimportant, which will allow them to recognize and seize upon what is of value and make the best of it. Teamwork allows them to expand their talents and achieve great things. Relationships, friendships, and partnerships represent interaction of a personal nature that is a source of valuable experience for number two people.

Number twos should cultivate and train their psychic abilities and extrasensory perception (ESP) in order to realize their dreams and visions with tenacity and discipline.

Crystals that support ambitions

Pearl* represents the Divine Mother and femininity in general. It helps us to discover our inner goddess and to develop and perfect attributes traditionally thought of as feminine, such as beauty, gentleness, and caring. Pearls bring us closer to the "self" and clarify feelings, helping us to resolve emotional difficulties, break down blockages, and dispel negative emotions.

---

* Pearls are generally available for sale as pendants, rings, or chains, and are rarely undrilled.

Affirmations

- I am wonderful and take pleasure in my life with joy in all its richness.
- I am aware of my feelings; I listen to my inner voice and trust my intuitive powers.
- I make decisions and act with certainty and resolution.

Other balancing and harmonizing crystals

With its iridescent spectrum of dancing colors, **noble opal** links us to the infinite variety of life.

Emerald brings us the gift of selfless love; it enhances our intuitive knowledge and brings a wider perspective and a deep understanding of our own life circumstances.

Crystal combination for number 2

A protective blend of healing crystals: four-way energetic protection for everyday use

Number two people quickly absorb negative vibrations from others or their environment, which makes spiritual/mental protection extremely important for them until they are able to stabilize themselves. The combination of crystals that follows is ideal. The four crystals can be worn on a chain, either individually or together, or employed to infuse and energize water and provide protection.

Black tourmaline, also known as schorl, is a classic protective crystal. It shields us from negative influences and thoughts, makes radiation more tolerable, reinforces boundary-setting, alleviates stress, and helps with tension and pain.

Rose quartz promotes emotional sensitivity and boosts empathy and our capacity for love and being ready to help. It brings spiritual energy, harmonizes negative vibrations, and relieves us of worries.

Chaorite helps to ward off negative influences of all kinds. It calms the nerves, reduces the power of external influences, and allows us to overcome constraints and resistance.

Clear quartz is a neutral source of energy that imparts strength and makes us less susceptible to unfavorable external influences. It stimulates the body's powers of self-healing and improves perception, making us clear-headed and aware, granting us positive life energy.

Healing effects on the body

Moonstone regulates the hormonal and lymphatic systems, enhances female fertility, and helps during puberty, the postnatal period, and throughout the menopause.

Rose quartz alleviates vein inflammation and thrombosis. It can be of help with psychosomatic heart conditions, diseases of the reproductive organs, neuritis (inflammation of the nerves), anxiety neurosis, and brain tumors. Rose quartz is also known as the crystal of love and is effective in instances of reduced libido and infertility. When used together, aventurine and rose quartz can help greatly with chronic insomnia.

Aventurine promotes calm during stress and alleviates heart conditions and skin complaints of a neurological origin; it lowers our cholesterol levels, helping with heart attack and arteriosclerosis. It also soothes the symptoms of asthma.

Carnelian eases rheumatism, sciatica, gout, and intestinal disorders. It helps to combat inflammation, blood poisoning, shingles, and varicose veins, and accelerates wound healing. It strengthens the circulation, heart, and kidneys, and accentuates the sense of touch.

Petrified wood calms the nerves and helps to protect against arteriosclerosis and narrowing of the arteries. It stimulates the metabolism and can be useful in combating excess weight and infection.

Prehnite removes toxins stored in our fat, alleviates the symptoms of asthma, and liver, kidney, and bladder conditions, and helps to prevent arteriosclerosis.

Pearl can be used in calcium deficiency, lumbago, sciatica, gout, allergies, weather sensitivity, and phlebitis (vein inflammation). It can also be effective against allergy to cat hair, psychosomatic anorexia, and cataracts. It provides support for the body's purification processes and excretory functions.

Noble opal supports our health in general, making us supple and full of vitality. It boosts heart, stomach, and bowel function, and the vision center in the brain.

Emerald has strong healing powers, alleviating inflammation, rheumatism, osteoporosis, sciatica, and flatulence, along with liver and gall bladder complaints. It boosts the vision, rejuvenates, regenerates, and combats memory loss.

The Number 3

Everyone has the facility to be creative,
only most people never notice it.
TRUMAN CAPOTE (AMERICAN WRITER)

Symbolism

The triangle is the symbol of the number 3. Three is the number of relaxation, creativity, and a zest for life, and of healing and transparency of emotions. It is also probably the most significant lucky number.

The interaction between opposites (such as between the numbers 1 and 2) creates something new, as is illustrated, for example, in the equation: father + mother = child.

Number 3's principal planet is **Jupiter**, a radiant, heavenly body thought to bring good fortune. It is the largest planet in our solar system and in mythology is associated with wisdom, victory, and justice. Jupiter symbolizes expansion, abundance, good luck, and success.

The healing crystal for 3

In ancient European cultures **blue topaz** was Jupiter's stone. Its energy helps us to identify goals that promise happiness and fulfillment, putting us in a cheerful and relaxed mood. Topaz also creates breakthroughs in spiritual development, promoting purity and clarity, banishing melancholy and gloomy thoughts. Stimulating energy flow and powers of self-healing, it combines mind, body, and soul in one. It makes our aura shine and allows us to experience the infinite.

Talents and Abilities

Number three people look facts squarely in the eye, roll up their sleeves and tackle issues with diligence and commitment. They are helpful, generous, intelligent, humorous, lively, and amiable. Always popular in company, they enjoy spending time with other people, talking and exchanging ideas. Communication is a key element of their personality. Their good mood and optimism are infectious. They have many talents and are hungry for knowledge, driven by curiosity and the desire to be creative. They like to engage in conversation, visit the theater, sing, dance, and enjoy the social whirl.

Sodalite helps to crystalize our thoughts and ideas. It encourages us to realize our goals, dispelling feelings of guilt and other blockages in our emotional life, freeing us from beliefs and subconscious patterns of behavior that hold us back. It reinforces our longing for true freedom and makes us focus on the essentials.

Ametrine is of real help when we transition into the New Age. It opens up our consciousness, unites opposing forces, and promotes harmony, optimism, and joy in life. This healing gemstone awakens spirituality and accelerates spiritual growth. It activates our creativity, allowing us to achieve our goals with great success. It also "deals us a lucky hand" by enabling us to do the right thing thanks to our intuition.

Amethyst quartz deepens our basic trust and reveals the meaning of life; it teaches us to trust our inner guidance with humility. As a stone of opposites, it combines in its violet color the red fire of vitality and the blue light of spirituality. It opens us up to the secrets of life in order to be able to fulfill our spiritual goals.

Sugilite is a crystal of happiness. It brings feelings of contentment, leading us out of the darkness and into the light. It helps us to maintain our own point of view and perspective and discover solutions that are based in acceptance. It teaches us how to find the Divine within ourselves.

Weaknesses

Number three people are often restless, mercurial, moody, and headstrong. They have a tendency to be sarcastic. Beauty, luxury, and pleasure are important to them. They attach greater importance to the external and appearances than to people. They do not take kindly to criticism and are slow to acknowledge their faults, which would represent failure, something they never allow in themselves. In their desire to be free, threes are extremely wasteful of their energies: they are soon enthused and start many more projects than they actually complete. They are high achievers, driven to succeed and keen to win, which often makes them come across as boastful and arrogant. Number three people are looking for love and recognition. They are willing to sacrifice a great deal to obtain these prizes, more than is good for them on some occasions.

Crystals that balance out weaknesses

Malachite brings awareness. It stimulates our inner world of images, delivering the gift of dreams and visions, bringing suppressed desires and needs to the surface while also making it easier to take decisions. This green gemstone helps us to recognize the darker elements of our emotional world, such as jealousy, envy, resentment, and greed. It creates inner and outer wealth with material possessions and emotional fulfillment, making our experience of life more intense.

Obsidian is a bearer of fiery, light-filled energy that it transmits to mind, body, and spirit, stimulating the emotions and the subconscious and opening closed doors within the very depths of our soul. It makes us aware of suppressed fears, conflicts, and traumas. When combined with clear quartz, it resolves conflicts swiftly, breaks down patterns of behavior that restrict us and helps us to accept criticism more easily. We can then assimilate all aspects of humanity within ourselves. This crystal brings honesty and reveals our own inner truth.

Covellite works on both a spiritual and physical level. It cleanses and purifies. It helps with feelings of discontent and false ambition. It helps us to leave behind old ways of behaving and negative experiences, allowing us to view the past in the correct light and to accept and love ourselves as we are. It reveals the significance and value of past events and provides support in dealing with many kinds of addiction.

Ambitions

The goal of number three people is to find the meaning of life, to recognize the world and the truth for what they really are. They wish to achieve unconditional love with confidence and trust, and to interpret the language of the heart. They love life and live it with great imagination and creativity.

Threes yearn for praise and admiration, but also for true love. They attract many with their impressive achievements and success and are able to transform discord into harmony thanks to their emotional strength and inner calm. Number three people should use their inventiveness, imagination, and creativity in all aspects of their lives and in all forms of artistic expression, including art, poetry, theater, singing, and language. This will enable them to share their sunny natures and enthusiasm with the world, allowing their personalities to mature and grow. Nature's gift is relaxation and balance. By being out in the natural world, enjoying its times of silence and simply living in the moment, we can sense a connection with our inner divine being and use this to live our lives in freedom and happiness. If they have the power to heal themselves, number three people can also heal those around them.

Crystals that support ambitions

Lapis lazuli is revered as a holy stone in many cultures. As a healing crystal associated with sovereigns and rulers, its energy allows us to be the "master of our own domain" once more. It forges a link with the human soul, allowing us to access new, higher dimensions. This crystal helps us to manage conflict, bringing harmony to our relationships and encouraging a search for truth, personal responsibility, prudence, and authenticity. In helping us to recognize higher connections, it is also a gemstone of wisdom.

Affirmations

- I am centered and focused; I use my talents and creative powers in a constructive manner.
- I trust my inner guidance and I activate the potential that lies within me.
- Good fortune is my companion and endless abundance and joy are by my side.

Other balancing and harmonizing crystals

Chrysocolla helps us to integrate spiritual insights into our lives. It grants us the gifts of honesty, trust, balance, and neutrality.

Selenite opens up our understanding of our own nature, makes our inner beauty shine, brings calm, peace, and serenity to those who need to relax, and helps us to withdraw from the hustle and bustle of the world to recharge our batteries in peace and quiet.

Healing effects on the body

Blue topaz helps to ease inflammation, heart pain, and skin rashes. It can also be useful for anorexia. It helps to alleviate stuttering and speech disorders.

Sodalite reduces high blood pressure and fever. It can help in instances of loss of voice and chronic hoarseness, reinforces the lymphatic system, and regulates the metabolism and glandular activity.

Ametrine can be used for eye complaints and hearing loss. It also restores balance to the autonomic nervous system and strengthens and reinvigorates the body after serious illness.

Amethyst quartz is effective against tension in and around the head and soothes migraine. It can be used to treat bumps and bruises, and it alleviates skin rashes, boils, and psoriasis. Helpful with menopausal symptoms, nervous conditions, and intestinal disorders, it also assists in the treatment of neurosis, hallucination, hysteria, and alcoholism.

Sugilite can be useful in cases of motor dysfunction, leukemia, epilepsy, and dyslexia. It provides support with severe toothache and can help during cancer therapy.

Malachite soothes cramp and is an effective treatment for headaches, menstrual complaints, whooping cough, sore muscles, phantom symptoms, and bedwetting.

Obsidian is recommended when we lose our inner vision of truth and so find it difficult to "see" in the outside world. It can support us throughout the associated purification process, relieving pain, tension, and vasoconstriction (narrowing of the blood vessels). It helps with the peripheral arterial disease known as "smoker's leg." It warms chronically cold hands and feet and accelerates tissue repair.

Covellite encourages body awareness, detoxifies connective tissue, provides support when trying to lose weight, and is also useful in cancer therapy.

Lapis lazuli can help with fever and muscle spasms. It is ideal for high blood pressure, complaints of the throat and difficulty with swallowing, along with wear of the intervertebral discs, phantom pain, and eye infection. It also alleviates psoriasis and depression and inhibits stroke and multiple sclerosis.

Chrysocolla is an excellent crystal for women. It calms and restores hormonal balance, assisting in menstrual complaints, premature birth, and miscarriage. It alleviates labor pain, high blood pressure, and fever. It also eases stomach and bowel disorders.

Selenite strengthens connective tissue and helps to alleviate all kinds of tension in the back and shoulders.

The Number 4

One day, everything will be well, That is our hope.
Everything's fine today, That is our illusion.
VOLTAIRE (FRENCH PHILOSOPHER)

Symbolism

Number 4 is the first earthly number, bringing both matter and space into being. We associate all things created by human hands with this number, hence its symbol is a square. It is the epitome of order, symbolizing classification and civilization on the one hand, and restraint and restriction on the other.

The principal planet of number 4 is **Uranus,** which governs the zodiac sign Aquarius. Uranus brings enlightenment and liberates the mind, representing community, experience, and equality. This form of freedom enables us to make room for the unexpected in life. Uranus encourages us to think in the abstract, in the form of images, and helps us to be intuitive and inventive; similarly, it shows us that restrictive social structures, beliefs, and old, fixed ways of thinking and behavior should be put behind us.

The healing crystal for 4

Garnet, the primal fire of life, is the gemstone of the bold and the brave, those who are being tested in their mission in life or by facing life's trials and tribulations. It helps us to cope with everyday life (giving us self-confidence, courage, and assurance) and brings success. It reinforces willpower, helping us to break away from established habits and patterns of behavior and offering protection from misfortune and danger. It fosters our visual imagination and can take us on the path to clairvoyance.

Talents and Abilities

Four is the number of stability and realization, and of the world and of matter. A karmic number, it represents reconciliation with the past. Within every problem lies an opportunity or the possibility of a challenge, and four sets a marker: all that is "sown" here, consciously or unconsciously, will be "reaped."

Number four people are born individualists, revolutionaries, and reformers, with uncompromising opinions and mentalities. They are skilled socially as well as being adept with technology, and are reliable, loyal, honest, direct, generous, and tolerant. Fours take great pleasure in learning and possess remarkably good memories, along with a powerful ability to concentrate. They think practically and are direct and sincere, patient and loyal. Helpful and punctual, they keep their promises, too.

Number fours love their homes, the natural world, and animals. Everything has a place and a value, and they go to great lengths to keep things that way. They consistently put into practice their desires and dreams in a methodical and practical manner. Number four people have both feet firmly on the ground and like to tread familiar paths. They are well aware of the value of money and have a thrifty mindset, avoiding risk and buying only what they really need. They are not gamblers; security is more important to them than risk.

Number fours strive for prosperity and do their utmost to achieve good results. Their professional lives are often associated with physical activity and they work hard and tirelessly. They stand out from the crowd for their healthy perspective on the world, good planning, and efficient organization, attributes that allow them to implement and realize their ideas and projects with speed. They make fair-minded business partners and require a secure and clearly structured (working) environment.

Crystals that boost talents and abilities

Green labradorite is a crystal of iridescent light. It fosters mediumship and intuition and helps us to grow spiritually through engaging with and coming to terms with our past. It shines a light on neglected talents and abilities and helps us to achieve our goals with creativity, imagination, and enthusiasm.

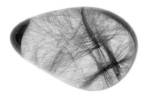

Rutilated quartz brings power and strength, providing support when we face challenges; it unravels entanglements and dispels fears. This healing gemstone opens doors and prompts a willingness to act. It shows us a positive way into the future, and brings a wealth of light and a readiness for new beginnings.

Weaknesses

Number four people are conservative and prefer to keep to what they know and trust, the things that have usually worked out for them in the past. Rather gloomy and depressive, they like to suffer and make a drama out of everything. They often give the impression of being loners and in so doing can cut themselves off from other people. Although fours frequently seem outwardly to be very sure of themselves, they can be hesitant and inhibited. They may appear very robust, but in fact are often unassuming and unobtrusive. They take feelings and emotions very seriously and generally find criticism deeply hurtful. They have a tendency to be harsh self-critics and to put themselves down. With their fixed opinions, they can also be stubborn and obstinate, and inclined toward sudden fits of anger. Their lives are made more difficult by their pessimism and pedantry, and they are often insensitive.

Crystals that balance out weaknesses

Zoisite helps to free us from a tendency to adapt to and accommodate the demands of others. It heals old wounds, balances out mood swings, and helps its wearer to realize their own dreams and desires. It promotes warm-heartedness and understanding. It is an excellent partnership crystal.

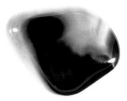

Sardonyx has the capacity to transform the negative emotions of rage, hatred, aggression, and fear. It points the way toward new solutions and can transmute karma and overcome sorrow.

Ambitions

Number four people aspire to live their daily lives with love, joy, and motivation. Their goal is to enjoy life, to avoid mistaken thinking, to balance the give-and-take in life, and to accept every living being on this planet without reservation or limitation. Number four people live well-organized, practical lives. It is important for them to demonstrate strength, security, and stability in the steady pursuit of their vocation and to achieve their high ambitions. They have very specific obligations to fulfill, both in a professional context and in their relationships with their fellow human beings. Once aware of these, they can think more clearly and reduce their focus on safety and security, while still keeping their life on solid foundations, bringing joy and exuberance into their lives. Spending time in the natural world will recharge their batteries, giving them new strength and vitality, while becoming aware that "the only security on Earth is to be found in reconciliation with oneself."

Turquoise* unites Heaven and Earth; it combines intuition with the power of the Earth. With its strong, powerful presence, turquoise helps us to penetrate the dream world more deeply. This gemstone allows us to recognize the root causes of the destinies that we impose upon ourselves and so shows us what we will "reap."

As a powerful protective crystal, turquoise keeps negative influences at bay. It reduces anxiety and fear of life, bringing fresh energy.

Aquamarine shines light and brings clarity into the hidden corners of the soul. It promotes spiritual growth, vision, and a sense

---

* Dyed magnesite is often sold in place of turquoise, so check the stone is genuine before buying.

of well-being, ease, and serenity. This crystal that is the color of water helps us to create order and bring unfinished cycles to an end. It brings clarity on an emotional level, making us sincere, dynamic, clear, and pure.

Azurite* opens the door to visions but also reveals what has made an impression on us and what belief patterns we have adopted. It promotes self-knowledge and spiritual development.

Affirmations

- I love my profession and carry out my work with ease and pleasure, accepting the help that comes my way.
- I am flexible and open to change and to new things.
- I am overcoming my focus on safety and security, and am transforming my ego.

---

* Azurite is usually sold as a natural rosette or a pendant.

Tree agate supports our strengths and provides security and stability. It energizes us and promotes endurance, makes us feel cheerful and happy, and helps with difficulty in learning and feelings of unrest and disquiet.

Mookaite is an earth crystal. It helps us to find our true identity, reinforces our sense of personal responsibility, and helps to overcome oppression and problems in relationships.

Andean opal guides us toward a new perspective on the future. It reinforces our aura, protects and shelters us, and brings great strength, promoting flexibility and adaptability.

Healing effects on the body

Red garnet stimulates the circulation, combating low energy, anemia, and bed sores. It also helps with erectile dysfunction, frigidity, venereal disease, arthritis, calcification, and a poor immune system.

Green labradorite alleviates rheumatism and gout, strengthens cells and nerves, and firms up skin tissue. It can also combat sensitivity to the weather, allergies, and inflammation.

Rutilated quartz provides support for diseases of the lungs and airways, and is very effective against fear and anxiety, neurosis, and tightness in the chest area; it stimulates cell regeneration and even promotes hair growth.

Zoisite helps to fight serious illness, inhibits inflammation, promotes fertility, boosts sexual performance, and is useful in complaints affecting the prostate, testes, and ovaries.

Sardonyx alleviates flu infection, cold sores, asthma, and thyroid problems; it facilitates the flow of bodily fluids and eases varicose veins.

Aquamarine is good for the lungs and airways and helps with whooping cough. It regulates hormonal balance, glandular problems, and nerve pain. It reinforces eyesight, boosts the liver, and alleviates allergies (hay fever, in particular).

Azurite fortifies the liver and gall bladder, stimulates the thyroid, improves the reactions, and bolsters the senses.

Tree agate boosts the kidneys and the immune system, encourages positive energy, and is an excellent crystal for children with ADHD and learning difficulties as it grounds the mind, regenerates, and calms.

Mookaite detoxifies skin tissue, boosts the liver, spleen, and pancreas, and helps with stomach and bowel complaints.

Andean opal detoxifies and cleanses the body, helps with water retention, and reinforces the immune system.

The Number 5

The ability to say the word "no"
is the first step to freedom.
NICOLAS CHAMFORT (FRENCH AUTHOR)

Symbolism

The number 5 is expressed in a pentagram, a five-pointed star. It represents the human being with four limbs and a head, as well as the four (earthly) elements and the "spirit." A five-pointed star is seen as a protective symbol that repels negative forces. The pentagram leads to unity, since it connects Heaven and Earth.

The principal planet for number 5 is **Mercury**, the smallest and fastest-moving planet in our solar system. It governs two zodiac signs, Gemini and Virgo. In mythology, Mercury is the messenger of the gods, a go-between who brought humans language, rhetoric, and the ability to communicate.

The healing crystal for 5

In the ancient world the **emerald** was seen as a crystal of divine inspiration. A very special healing gemstone, its green energy permeates, cleanses, and heals both our aura and our entire energy system. It helps us to leave behind negative childhood experiences and frees us from damaging energies, emotional bottlenecks, and blockages. Emerald infuses us with gentleness, love, and peace, rejuvenating and enhancing our appearance.

This gemstone also promotes clairvoyance and prescience. It makes us sincere and purposeful; it brings our bodies, thoughts, emotions, and actions into alignment and harmony. Emerald also helps us to overcome fate, conveying a sense of security and leading us toward the light.

Talents and Abilities

Number 5 represents freedom and communication, symbolizing a pure spirit. Number five people are sociable, multitalented, flexible and adaptable, and love life's infinite variety. They like to travel and discover new places and people, with the result that they always have interesting tales to tell.

Fives are full of life and positivity. They have an intensely dynamic aura of success and are "pure energy." They love to experience the unconventional and are always on the hunt for new interests, stimuli, changes, and challenges. Personal freedom is one of life's necessities for them.

Number fives are sensitive, sensuous, and romantic creatures. Their sympathetic, intelligent, dynamic manner makes them very popular, and they enjoy long and deep friendships. They display an interest in a wide variety of topics and are curious about life. Number fives exert an almost magical attraction on the opposite sex, which can lead to conflict.

Fives are also artistically talented, easily enthused, and are both active and spontaneous. With generous hearts, they are keen to help their fellow human beings and like taking on charitable responsibilities. They are intelligent, impulsive, and quick-witted. They love contact with people (in groups), set great store by their own outward appearance, and always want to make a good impression. As keen readers, skilled orators, and multiskilled organizers, number five people are entertaining conversational partners. They are quick on the uptake, adept at thinking ahead and acting with speed.

Bubbling with ideas, they are happy to take on several things at once. They can often achieve more alone than an entire team working together.

Crystals that boost talents and abilities

Blue-banded chalcedony has long been associated with orators and the act of speaking. With its energy, it helps number five people to communicate and achieve their ambitions. It removes inhibitions about speaking out, releases blockages in and around the neck and throat, and instills calm in moments of particular strain or nervous tension. It brings serenity, opening us up to inner inspiration. Chalcedony provides support when we feel weak, sad, or discontented. It provides access to our intuitive subconscious knowledge and helps us to express this in words. It promotes lightness, vitality, and optimism, and so intensifies our pleasure at meeting others.

Weaknesses

Number five people often get lost in the vast choice of options and ideas that life has to offer, and instead they can feel empty inside. To avoid addressing this, they prefer to busy themselves with events in the outside world. Fives are passionate collectors of all kinds of material things and love to accumulate knowledge, reading books and attending seminars in the hope of filling the void. They are ruled more by their heads and their minds and are less concerned with matters of the heart. They do not mind breaking rules and accept advice grudgingly. They are easily bored by the repetition and drudgery of daily life. Fives are fussy, restless, and impatient people who often seem under pressure. They are easily distracted and prefer to have "a finger in many pies." They can be moody, pessimistic, grumpy, unreliable, impulsive, and restless. Their quick temper can easily lead to outbursts of rage, which then blow over just as promptly. Rapid mood swings complicate their relationships in all aspects of their lives.

Green moss agate helps us to become more open and tolerant and to remain grounded. It brings spiritual freedom, inspiration, and an ability to communicate. This healing gemstone boosts consciousness, reinforces intellectual abilities, and dispels fear and fixed ideas. It helps us to be at one with our true feelings and to get in touch with our softer, childlike side. Moss agate also stimulates personal responsibility and introduces balance and harmony.

Tiger's eye brings the gifts of warmth, good fortune, and a sense of safety. It helps us to realize that true fulfillment, security, and trust in life lie within us. It demonstrates that life is in a constant state of flux, bringing courage, confidence, and drive.

*"People who merely function are missing out on
the adventure of life."*
ARMIN MUELLER-STAHL (GERMAN ACTOR)

Ambitions

Number five people want the personal freedom to live their lives and to do what makes them happy, regardless of what other people may think. Their goal is to overcome life's hurdles without any problem, to be entirely free and to think more with their heart rather than their head.

It is important for number five people to be fully aware of their feelings and to broaden their horizons where necessary, and not to settle for lazy compromises. It is also important for fives to experience freedom in both thought and deed, to tear down old political, societal, social, and economic structures. They should not subscribe exclusively to a single teacher or guru, as there will be many. Their professional competence and skills attract those in need of help and advice, and they can perform miracles with their infectious enthusiasm. Finding harmony in feelings, actions, and self-expression leads to independence and brings true freedom in life. Fives will only achieve their true goal when they seek and find the truth within themselves and accept that their longing can only be satisfied by connecting with their inner selves.

Sodalite establishes the strongest of links between mind and matter. It helps us to remain loyal to our aspirations and goals. With its energy, we can adapt our ideas and make them reality. This gemstone heals wounds left by relationships, eases the path of breakups, and provides particular support for those who feel they have been left alone. Sodalite gives us the strength and energy to consciously discard past behaviors and beliefs in order to open up to new paths. It can also be used to counteract fear of any kind. Sodalite helps vivacious number five people to find silence and to engage with the natural world with love and respect.

Affirmations

- I see the wisdom in my heart, and I forge a link between the feelings of my heart and my rational thinking.
- I am in the here and now, free in my thoughts; I am in the flow of life, and things will turn out for the best.
- I welcome harmony and joy into my life, and I accept what happens to me with divine trust.

Charoite helps us to engage with change and overcome obstacles in our way; it boosts the memory, protects us from taking wrong decisions, and mitigates the power of external influences. Charoite also promotes restful sleep and creative dreams.

Heliotrope belongs to the jasper family. It is an earth crystal that allows us to recognize and identify our own strengths and weaknesses. It helps our sense of self to shield from undesirable influences. It brings calm where there is irritability, impatience, or aggression.

Aragonite has a calming effect, introducing stability when life is moving too fast. It reinforces a person's male aspects and qualities.

Healing effects on the body

Emerald is a stone of regeneration and rejuvenation. It boosts eyesight (and helps with eye conditions), combats sinusitis, flu, and rheumatism, and can be effective for poor memory, flatulence, and complaints of the gall bladder, heart, and liver.

Blue-banded chalcedony helps to combat hoarseness, swollen lymph glands, sensitivity to weather, vocal cord issues, diseases of the airways, water retention in the tissues, and nervous tension. It is also used to combat the symptoms of the menopause.

Sodalite calms the nervous system, lowers blood pressure, helps with asthma and loss of voice, and provides support for problems affecting the throat and larynx.

Charoite eases pain and cramp and as such is popular as a complementary therapy to cancer treatments. It also stimulates our basic metabolism and calms the nerves.

Green moss agate reinforces the immune system and is extremely helpful against a dry cough, bronchitis, and other infections, as it stimulates lymph flow.

Tiger's eye alleviates asthma, nervous tension and pain, while also reinforcing bones, joints, and vision.

Heliotrope is good for the immune system and helps with rheumatism; it detoxifies and deacidifies.

Aragonite is used to treat problems with the intervertebral discs and degenerative rheumatism; it also boosts the immune system.

The Number 6

If love does not know how to give and take without restrictions, it is not love, but a transaction.
EMMA GOLDMAN (AMERICAN PEACE ACTIVIST)

Symbolism

Six is represented by the hexagram, the six-pointed star. This symbol combines opposites: mind and matter, light and darkness, time and space, fire and water, man and woman. When we are able to unite these opposites, we can possess significant healing powers, channeling and grounding energy from the higher planes of light. Six represents feminine, spiritual, and unconditional love.

The principal planet of number six people is **Venus**. It governs the zodiac signs Taurus and Libra and our personal value systems. It provides harmony and balance.

The healing crystal for 6

Chrysocolla is of particular significance in these times of change. It bears wisdom and purity within itself, bringing trust and honesty to those who wear it and making them aware of their emotions and needs. Chrysocolla combines understanding and feeling, giving its wearers renewed energy. It has a particular connection with the infinite, and so brings a wonderful sense of openness to life with the gifts of peace and compassion, balance and empathy. With its divine vibrations, we can live with unconditional love.

Talents and Abilities

Six is the number of vitality and assertiveness. It represents self-love and devotion to our fellow human beings.

All that is maternal and feminine, tenderness, reliability, and empathy, can be found in the number 6. Number six people are helpful, conscientious, and socially engaged. They bring a sense of safety, security, and protection. As friendly, fair, and unpartisan advisors, they provide understanding and guidance to those seeking help in assessing the rights and wrongs of a given situation. Sixes are social individuals who stand up for truth, justice, and order. They are forward-looking and courageous, with a sixth sense for danger. They are practical by nature, aware of their responsibilities, impartial, unbiased, and loyal.

Number six people approach their tasks and endeavors with intelligence, understanding, and clear emotions. Their plans are underpinned by a strongly developed intuition that also gives them the necessary insight. They enjoy the recognition of working in caring professions or advisory roles. Most people like sixes and feel good in their company as they are friendly, charming, optimistic, patient, conscientious, and tolerant. They have a pronounced personal aura, eroticism, and sensuality, bringing calm, attention, love, and understanding to those around them. They are excellent hosts and like to be surrounded by beauty; they like to decorate their homes with style and taste and enjoy the world of esthetics and the arts. The find relaxation in music and rhythm.

Crystals that boost talents and abilities

Moqui marbles (limonite balls) are available in pairs. They strengthen partnerships, encourage a happy marriage, help us to attract a soulmate, and show us what our souls long for: the love of our lives. Moqui marbles bring warmth and relaxation to the body, making it easier to get to sleep.

Morganite is a powerful gemstone for the heart. It can help to heal heartbreak and enables us to realize that everything that we seek in another person, we can only experience within ourselves. This healing crystal eases the pressure caused by stress, ambition, and the expectations that are placed upon us, making time for leisure and relaxation instead.

Weaknesses

Number six people succumb easily to self-doubt and as a result can be wary and distrustful. They treat praise and recognition with caution, on the assumption that people are using flattery to get on their good side. In matters of belief, number six people tend to be blinkered by their innately conservative and realistic natures. They find it difficult to make decisions, their spiritual growth generally being hampered by a deep-seated need for support and safety. If things go wrong, they look for a scapegoat right away and want everything set out in "black and white." Their composure is easily upset by small things and making choices is never easy for them. Number six people will become involved in a fierce argument once in a while, but they can also shy away from confrontation. Their deep yearning for love can make sixes too passionate, and they can become possessive and jealous, or indeed overwhelm others emotionally. Sixes may also be susceptible to various dependencies and addictions, such as food, alcohol, smoking, and drugs. They may also find computers and sport addictive.

Aventurine has a gentle and conciliatory effect, soothing the emotions. It balances our moods and feelings and restores inner harmony, calming us during moments of anger or fury. This gemstone can also deliver a sense of joy and serenity.

Epidote/unakite is a crystal of regeneration at every level. It can help to smooth over potential problems in a mother and child relationship. It also clears and strengthens the lower chakras, stabilizes the aura, and straightens the spine. It brings strength and assertiveness.

Ambitions

Number six people value their homes and their families highly. Love and sexuality are important issues for them. Their aim is to accept all living creatures as they are—animal, plant, or human—in order to live in peace and harmony.

It is important for them to express their love for humanity and for every living creature. They can forge deep emotional connections and are ready to help their fellow human beings. They are generous with their support when it is required and expect nothing in return. Sixes are happy and in harmony with the Divine when they are able to stand up for their ideals and stand by their decisions.

Inner balance is absolutely essential for sixes. When among a group of people, just their mere presence has a healing effect thanks to their ability to listen and understand. They want to love, teach, and serve others, to bring comfort to humankind. Love and empathy are their highest spiritual values. Number six people go with the flow of life and in so doing experience how strength, courage, and love increase more and more. They attract people whose needs and desires they can help to fulfill with light and healing.

Rose quartz is a love crystal. It helps us to engage with others freely, openly, and without expectations. Its aura gives our hearts room to breathe. It promotes tenderness, love of ourselves and our neighbors, and a romantic, helpful, and open-minded nature.

The pink light of rose quartz helps us to rediscover happiness and fulfillment. It removes worry and makes us receptive to music, painting, and creative writing.

Malachite has had a sacred association with goddesses in all cultures. It represents beauty, friendship, sensuousness, esthetics, and the musical arts. It is a conduit for all things feminine. With its swirling patterns of light and dark green, malachite shows how light and shadow complement each other and in doing so reveals what we need for our own positive development. It helps us to accept ourselves as we are, to create balance between feelings and understanding, and to solve issues in our heart chakra. It grants the gifts of renewal, transformation, and a deep love of life. Malachite assists in furthering our development and in identifying and resolving blockages in our subconscious.

Affirmations

- I let go of old ways of thinking and past influences, and I accept that everyone has their own life, opinions, and views.
- I stand up for my convictions, make my own decisions, and find honest, creative solutions.
- I listen to the voice of my heart and am in harmony with myself.

Other balancing and harmonizing crystals

Pyrite groups are crystals of healing and integration for those who feel excluded and misunderstood. They promote self-knowledge and help us to acknowledge our darker side. They combat fear and depression and ease chronic tiredness. Pyrite cubes particularly support those who are physically or mentally disadvantaged. They shake the soul awake and bring new strength and hope.

Amber provides support in good times and bad. Its maternal properties give confidence, independence, and protection to those who have had to grow up without a mother's love.

Healing effects on the body

Chrysocolla is a very good crystal for women. It alleviates menstrual complaints, helps to prevent miscarriage and premature birth, combats infection, relaxes the digestive tract, lowers blood pressure, and regulates thyroid function.

Moqui marbles are regeneration crystals and can be used for chronic complaints, improving blood flow and boosting the skin's protective properties.

Morganite inhibits arteriosclerosis and acts positively on disorders of the heart, nervous conditions, and impotence.

Aventurine has a healing effect on skin complaints, rashes, eczema and conditions affecting the heart that are linked to the emotions. It lowers cholesterol levels and reinforces connective tissue.

Epidote/unakite supports the body's healing processes; it also strengthens the liver and gall bladder and the entire immune and digestive systems.

Rose quartz helps with psychosomatic heart conditions, venereal disease, and sexual difficulties, as well as with phlebitis and thrombosis.

Malachite can be placed on painful or ailing areas of the body. It relieves colic, cramps, menstrual complaints, and asthma, and helps in instances of poisoning, rheumatism, and poor sight.

Pyrite cubes should be seen as a mirror with which we can identify the causes of issues and then find solutions.

Amber promotes the self-healing process and is of help with asthma, whooping cough, bronchitis, flu, and stomach and bowel complaints. It relieves teething pain in toddlers and helps to soothe aching joints.

The Number 7

Men are wise in proportion not to their experience, but to their capacity for experience.
GEORGE BERNARD SHAW (IRISH PLAYWRIGHT)

Symbolism

The symbol of number 7 is the menorah, the seven-branched candelabra used in Jewish worship. It symbolizes enlightenment—the 7 pillars of wisdom. The candelabra's 7 branches indicate our location, as well as the 4 points of the compass, and the directions up and down. The number 7 comprises number 3 (the number of heaven, the soul, and all that is masculine) and number 4 (the number of Earth, all that is human, and all that is feminine); it connects both God and man. It is therefore the number of wholeness and the emotional maturity that unites mind, body, and spirit.

The principal planet of number 7 is **Neptune**, which governs the zodiac sign of Pisces. In the mythology of ancient Rome, Neptune was the god of the sea. Neptune slowly and relentlessly breaks down all the barriers that the ego erects around itself. Its role in psychological terms is to help us overcome our limitations by refining our feelings and allowing our emotional life to evolve on a continuous basis.

Amethyst quartz was known for its sobering and clarifying effects even in ancient times. Its gentle vibrations bring a calmness that allays fears, rage, and inhibitions so that the mind can open up to new experiences. It promotes lasting spiritual wakefulness and a sense of spirituality; it reinforces our sense of justice and critical faculties, and encourages honesty, sincerity, and clarity. It helps us to deal with loss and sorrow and assists us in finding deep inner peace. This violet crystal clarifies the mind's eye, increases concentration, and brings the gifts of visions and pleasant dreams. It promotes inspiration and intuition, opening us up to the secrets of life. When we accept its guidance, it will point us toward our real mission and purpose in life. It can gather old energies and transform them, prompting selflessness in the actions and thoughts of those who wear it. It encourages us to overcome attachments, repetitive habits and behaviors that we find it difficult to control, and addictive behavior. It is also used for all problems caused by stress, nervous tension, and great strain.

Talents and Abilities

Seven is the number of mysticism and fullness in life. Number seven people are constantly searching for inner knowledge and the meaning of life.

Sevens are considered conscientious, loyal, respectful, and diligent. They are skilled at organizing, planning, managing, and developing projects, and lead the way in virtually every domain. They very much dislike fuss and bother. For seven people, life is ruled by unexpected change; the highs and lows of their lives leave deep marks upon them as they are very sensitive, natural, and warm. They are charming and have a sound insight into human nature. Sevens are inquisitive and keen to learn, with a natural leaning toward religion, philosophy, metaphysics, and spirituality. They are fascinated by psychological and philosophical studies. Seven people want to see, experience, and understand everything, to get to the bottom of complex questions and problems. Their keen powers of observation help them to analyze every situation. They listen to their inner voice and thus have the ability to get to grips with what really lies behind things, the real causes. They are also receptive to everything intellectual, to knowledge and education. They prefer to keep other people at arm's length in order to think and philosophize. Peace and calm are as essential for seven people as the air that they breathe. They make trustworthy friends and reliable partners and are sympathetic and honest. Seven people treat others with respect and have fellow feeling with all creatures—they love nature and animals.

Falcon eye brings spiritual reorientation. It frees us from confused thinking and brings clarity that allows us to understand the greater connections in life; it shows our reasoning mind what is harming our soul. Falcon eye combats the ego, helps bring about mental stability, fosters our intuition and perceptiveness, and protects us from difficult situations and false friends.

Ametrine gives us the strength to stop hiding behind illness, fears, and problems; it clarifies everything that is unclear. It gives us the power to act and to do what is possible.

Weaknesses

Number seven people are pessimists and volatile, often refusing to accept something as a matter of principle. They may be serious, introverted, and reticent, and may therefore be perceived as loners. Sevens are reserved and distrustful, feeling ill at ease in groups, with a tendency toward self-isolation. They don't like listening to advice and find it hard to accept; they also tend to put off unpleasant tasks. They don't like to get involved with emotional problems and would prefer not to acknowledge mental pain or to see that life can have a darker side. Number seven people like to give the impression that they are cheerful but are often sad deep down, deceiving both themselves and those around them. They often smile, even when things are going badly. Sevens generally hide their emotions and thoughts, and are often unsure of themselves, feeling misunderstood and alone. They are neither adaptable nor domestically inclined and seek in their surroundings what is missing from within them.

Orange calcite is the ideal crystal for those who no longer believe in the positive things in life. It promotes our ability to organize and plan, encourages self-confidence and steadfastness, and improves the memory, bringing the gifts of basic trust and a smile with which to greet every day. Orange calcite helps us find a way to make sense of life.

Prehnite is a revitalizing crystal that is useful in combating dark and depressive feelings or neuroses. It has a gentle effect and is good for those who are wary of healing, allowing those who wear it to open up. It provides support against low mood and makes people enterprising and more cheerful.

Ambitions

The most important issue for seven people is basic trust—to allow themselves to be guided by their intuition, to trust in the path their life takes, and to accept life as it is. Silence and meditation help us along the conscious path to what is inside us. All knowledge and all wisdom can be found in every human being. The goal for seven people is to have a clear direction in life, in other words, to find truth within their hearts and to realize that the material world is illusion and the spiritual plane reality.

Everything that sevens experience in the outside world is a reflection of themselves within, so only what is already present within can be reflected. The cleansing of feelings is therefore important, checking their behavior and attitudes to make sure they progress in life in these respects. Number seven people like to engage with philosophy, religion, and metaphysics, and are eager for self-knowledge. When they look for answers, they do so far from the "madding crowd," discovering their own philosophy, one by which they can live. To find our inner light, we sometimes have to first withdraw from the outside world, in order to return to the present reality with greater strength. Sevens have a natural instinct for the truth. Their powerful and balanced intuition lends them the necessary insight and helps them to make decisions, and to plan and create projects. It is important for sevens to trust their vision and to rely on their intuition for stability, to ground themselves in order to be aware of their own strengths, and to bring clarity into their lives, thus achieving greater wisdom.

With its delicate violet-pink coloration, **kunzite** makes sublime love resonate within us. It has a strong influence on the soul and helps us to grow spiritually and to express the inexhaustible source of love and joy to the outside world. It is a great help where there is mental suffering, dispelling fear. Bringing the gift of divine trust, it allows us to carry out tasks in devotion and humility, without losing sight of ourselves.

Azurite possesses very powerful energy and so is not necessarily recommended for inexperienced users. For those who are able to handle its great power, this crystal is ideal for opening up the doors of perception to our inner visions and dreams and for making contact with our souls. It promotes consciousness and self-knowledge and is of principal importance for our spiritual development. Combining **azurite** with **malachite** is also of interest, as the latter similarly helps us gain access to higher spheres.

Affirmations

- I bring my own truth to light; I act consciously and according to the best of my knowledge.
- I am connected to the source within me; I am safe and secure and I know that all power resides within me.
- I find a place of security within me and feel safe and protected.

Other balancing and harmonizing crystals

Silver eye serpentine helps us to maintain boundaries and protects us against all that is negative; it balances out mood swings, calms our stress, and allows us to find inner peace. It is an important crystal when we are dogged by grim thoughts and constant existential angst. It teaches us to live in love.

Prasem quartz (prase) or **seriphos green quartz** soothes aggression, rage, and fits of anger; it promotes persistence, serenity, and calm, as well as self-control and self-determination. **Silver eye serpentine** and **prasem quartz** are highly suitable for use as meditation crystals; ideal partner crystals in this respect include **falcon eye** and **petrified wood**.

Healing effects on the body

Amethyst quartz helps to combat insomnia, headaches, and all kinds of skin problems, as well as boils, bruises, and swellings. It regulates the pancreas and gut flora.

Falcon eye boosts our eyes and vision and is effective against nervous tension and tremors. It also mitigates hormonal hyperfunction.

Ametrine is good for convalescence after serious illness; it stimulates brain activity, promotes cell metabolism, and cleanses tissue.

Orange calcite stimulates the metabolism of calcium, increases energy levels, promotes digestion, boosts low blood pressure, and reinforces bone and body tissue.

Prehnite helps us to eliminate the toxins deposited in body fat and detoxifies the body; it boosts liver, bladder, and kidney function.

Kunzite is exceptionally effective against the symptoms of sciatica, neuralgia, and nervous complaints; it regulates thyroid function while also helping with back and heart conditions.

Azurite reinforces the immune system, helps to dissolve gallstones, and improves our reactions.

Azurite and malachite help with liver function and have a detoxifying and antispasmodic effect against conditions affecting women; they can be used to dissolve ulcers and tumors.

Serpentine (silver eye serpentine) is a powerfully protective crystal; it will also repel parasites, insects, and ticks, and alleviate muscle cramps and migraine.

Prasem quartz is good for bruises, swelling, sunburn, and sunstroke; it is also effective for short sight and cataracts.

The Number 8

Pay attention to the little things in the world—
they make life richer and more content.

CARL HILTY (SWISS LAY THEOLOGIAN)

Symbolism

Number 8's symbol is a double closed loop known as a lemniscate. The symbol of infinity and eternity, it is the threshold for a new beginning at a "higher" level. It marks the crossing point from the old to the new, to better, greater things. Eight is also the number of justice, balance, and fulfillment. Just like zero (0), it has no beginning or end, but crosses in the center. It enables us to understand the significance of all aspects of our personal development—physical, mental, and spiritual.

Eight is a karmic number, where we process things within the unconscious and prepare for the transformation brought about by the number 9.

The principal planet of number eight people is **Saturn**, which governs the zodiac sign of Capricorn. It symbolizes that we reap what we sow. It embodies justice and the dynamic of cause and effect. Saturn demands clarity, form, and structure; it represents concentration on what is essential. It creates order by continually bringing us back down to earth with facts and reminds us of our obligations. By taking on responsibility and showing discipline in our self-realization, we can learn more and continue our development.

The **sapphire** is known as Saturn's gemstone; it is also the stone of belief and peace of mind. It is a powerful protective crystal and will help those who wear it to find their way along their spiritual path and toward their own divinity. It leads us away from what is superficial in life and from wanting to "have it all." This healing crystal removes confusion and dispels illusions as we follow our destiny. It promotes a love of truth and guides us calmly and attentively toward our life's goal.

Talents and Abilities

Number eight people are authoritative and influential, radiating strength, power, leadership potential, and success. They are involved at the highest levels in the business world and like to have everything under control.

Having set high ethical standards for themselves and others, they set their sights on substantial goals, doing their very best and expecting the same from their peers. Eights are known for their generosity, recognizing and honoring good performance.

They love the world of business, money, and wealth, using their strong will, great energy, and powers of concentration to obtain these and be successful. They are practical, energetic, hardworking, and quick. Number eight people show great self-discipline and decisiveness, with an instinct for investment, speculation, and financial matters. They are creative in devising and implementing their plans and ideas. New challenges drive them on, as only new experiences lend w-"eight" to their arguments. They are interesting and fascinating people, true epicureans who enjoy all the good things that life has to offer. They love status symbols and want to have sufficient material possessions to be able to lead a pleasant life. They have a particularly strong instinct for art, form, color, sounds, and fragrance. Number eight people are also emotional and are good at courting popularity.

Crystals that boost talents and abilities

Black tourmaline, also known as **schorl**, is considered the strongest protective crystal. It protects from avarice, power, disloyalty, and other negative influences, and penetrates into the deepest blockages to clear them. This healing crystal stimulates in us openness, freshness, and clarity. It brings the gift of a zest for life and self-confidence and reinforces our ability to achieve goals that are in harmony with the divine plan. Black tourmaline also promotes discipline and perseverance, helping us to achieve abundance and prosperity.

Weaknesses

Like the number 4, number 8 is a karmic number. Life brings many challenges and number eight people have to undergo many highs and lows in order to experience harmony. They often seem impatient, aloof, and dismissive, and they do not like to conform. They can be rebellious, tyrannical, and unfeeling. They enjoy their power and are equally able to wield it to negative effect. Their path to success is through the kind of hard work that is generally associated with overcoming many obstacles and disappointments. Eights are very intensely wrapped up in themselves and often give the impression of being closed and unapproachable. They can be rude and impatient with people they do not consider important, and they admit to having feelings only reluctantly. They are self-righteous and find it hard to admit mistakes, let alone to apologize for them. They would like to be perfect and also to appear as such to the outside world. They are dogmatic, always seeing faults in others, and are disinclined to admit their own weaknesses. Eights can draw important insights from the reflections of others.

Rhodonite is also known as "rescue crystal;" it has a reassuring, constructive effect, promoting understanding and forgiveness. It helps us to resolve conflict in a spirit of light and love, bringing reconciliation and peace. Rhodonite soothes us when we feel wounded mentally and emotionally, while also allaying fears and feelings of panic. It helps us to remain clear and alert, even in extreme situations and when under great stress. It is very effective on a physical level, guiding us toward health and a new lease of life. Rhodonite has a soothing effect when we feel confused or have experienced trauma or a shock of some kind. It helps us to remain calm and act reasonably in the face of provocation and insult, or when we desire revenge.

Magnesite is a powerful relaxation crystal. It has a calming effect and can be used to combat fear, irritability, and nervous tension, helping those who wear it to accept and love themselves. It promotes serenity and the ability to be flexible and compliant.

Apache tears, also known as smoky obsidian, help us to let go. They soothe sadness, sorrow, and feelings of guilt, alleviate depression, allay fears for the future, and bring the gift of new courage with which to face life. With apache tears we can experience healing and redemption and can accept the gift of grace.

Ambitions

The goal of number eight people is to navigate their way through life comfortably and with fairness. For eights, business and trade should be associated with truth and justice, which are important issues for them.

When number eight people are able to relinquish outdated patterns of thinking and behavior, and feelings of guilt and self-condemnation, they can focus on their spiritual development, learning to accept and love themselves. Their goal is to forgive and excuse their fellow human beings, to bring their strengths to bear in a positive way, and to live out their deepest essential purpose. Forgiveness is a form of conflict resolution, but it should come instinctively from deep within the heart, with unconditional love and humility, rather than as a result of thinking things through. When number eights accept accept that everything that happens to them is a part of the divine order and exerts an influence on their personal development, they can learn to be grateful for both their positive and negative experiences. "You reap what you sow." Problems in life should be viewed as an opportunities to learn. If eights can overcome their desire for comfort and convenience, they can escape their feelings of sorrow and suffering and live a comfortable and harmonious life.

Number eight people should open their hearts and be ready to trust themselves, and in doing so also learn to trust others. If they combine their strengths with their spirituality and use their talents thoughtfully and wisely, they can achieve their goals through persistence and steadfastness and with enthusiasm, while staying true to themselves.

Fluorite promotes spiritual development and is also known as the "crystal of genius." It helps us to structure our thoughts and process information and is therefore an ideal crystal to help with study and concentration. It sharpens our powers of discrimination, opens ours hearts, lightens our mood, and brings balance. **Rainbow fluorite** has incredible presence, bringing harmony to the mind, body, and spirit, and sparking vitality and feelings of great happiness.

Celestite* is a wonderful crystal for promoting optimism and confidence. Its power can be likened to the energy of a diamond and it gives us a sense of how fulfilled and happy we could actually be.

---

* Celestite exists mainly in druse form; it can be usefully arranged in rooms as it stimulates the human subconscious and can emit so many positive impulses.

It brings the gift of inner wealth, makes things clear and pure, and attracts energies that have a positive effect on the financial aspects of life.

Affirmations

- I love my work and my life; I take full responsibility for it and rely on my intuition.
- I strike a balance between private happiness and professional success.
- I have all the money, time, and help that I need right now, as I attract material prosperity and spiritual fullness.

Other balancing and harmonizing crystals

Sunflower quartz helps us to bring order to the profound depths of the soul, penetrating energetic barriers, boosting self-awareness, and providing deep insights into life and the past. Sunflower quartz can also be used to connect with the power of our ancestors.

Amazonite helps us to let go of the idea that we are victims of fate; it compensates for extreme mood swings, easing sorrow and grief. This healing crystal is especially good for Indigo children.

Apatite brings vitality and openness and the gift of variety in life; it helps us to overcome stress, listlessness, and exhaustion.

Healing effects on the body

Sapphire lowers fever and blood pressure and is effective against skin blemishes and skin conditions, and excessive sweating, sciatica, and mood swings.

Black tourmaline (schorl) can be used to help sharpen the sense of smell, and to combat neurosis and all kinds of pain and energy blockages.

Rhodonite helps heal internal and external injuries, stomach ulcers, and scar tissue, and can help with multiple sclerosis and autoimmune illnesses.

Magnesite provides support for all dental issues, and helps with migraine, colic, and leg cramp; it can have beneficial protective effects for the heart.

Apache tears (Smoky obsidian) strengthen vision, relieve topical pain, sprains, and back problems.

Fluorite can have a protective effect against mental illness and forges a link between the left and right halves of the brain. It may mitigate the symptoms associated with asthma and allergies, and has a regenerating effect on teeth, bones, hair, and nails.

Celestite provides support during convalescence, dissolves calluses in tissue and bone, and is extremely effective against muscle stiffness.

Sunflower quartz is good for dry skin, dry eyes and helps lymph flow.

Amazonite soothes cramps, harmonizes the pituitary gland and thymus, and regulates metabolic disorders.

Apatite is beneficial for the skeleton; it helps with the formation of bone, cartilage, and teeth. It is also good for joint pain, arthrosis, and rickets.

The Number 9

*Love is the strongest force the world possesses and yet
it is the humblest imaginable.*

MAHATMA GANDHI (INDIAN FREEDOM FIGHTER)

Symbolism

The energies of all the numbers 0–8 are reflected in number 9. Its symbol is a spiral, one of the oldest symbols of all and is a representation of the unity of mind, body, and spirit. Nine is a holy number that represents transformation. As the final single-digit number in the sequence, it symbolizes crossing over onto a new plane, a higher level, a higher space, a higher consciousness. It is the number of initiation, of ascension to a higher level of being. It remains loyal to itself and endures forever. Number nine people therefore have a relationship with the Divine Source of everything that was, is, and will be, whatever form that may take.

Number 9's principal planet is **Mars**, which governs the zodiac sign Aries and helps us to achieve our goals, stand up for our convictions and desires, and fulfill our expectations in the outside world. Mars is certain, resolute, full of energy, courage, and drive, and is an object lesson in how to assert an independent personality in the world. The planet **Pluto** also plays an important role for the number 9; it is here we encounter far-reaching processes of change, whose aim is to allow us to grow beyond ourselves and unite with the greater whole.

Jasper* is found in a number of forms and is often described as the "mother of all crystals." The jasper family therefore helps to ground people, bringing courage, strength, vitality, renewed spirit, heart, and understanding. Jasper cleanses thoughts and feelings, and alleviates nervous tension, unease, rash behavior, and aimlessness. It also brings wisdom, with a purifying and protective vital energy, and teaches altruism, modesty, and patience, reinforcing our intentions to do good.

Talents and abilities

Nine is the number of empathy, of all-encompassing love, a love of all creation and all people. Number nine people are aware that the highest form of love is when we act on an unconditional basis, without expecting anything in return.

Since all numbers are contained within 9, it is more diverse than the other numbers. It brings great responsibility and extraordinary

---

* The best known of the various kinds of jasper are red, yellow, and green jasper, although picture jasper and leopardskin jasper are also available.

opportunities. Nines have strong characters and enormous self-assurance. Viewed as powerful, courageous, just, and generous, they are also diligent, inventive, and highly talented in almost every field. Nines accept new beginnings and change, while their intuition allows them to make the right choice or decision spontaneously. With the ability to think logically, they can express themselves very well in both spoken and written language, as well as with their body language. They are good—if rather glib—listeners. Blessed with artistic gifts, they have a natural interest in philosophy and spirituality. Number nines also have an excellent understanding of people and are true philanthropists. They are highly sensitive, charismatic, farsighted, magnanimous, optimistic, and wise. The courage, fortitude, and decisiveness that they demonstrate, not to mention their desire to be of help, make them great protectors. Their friendships, relationships, and marriages are frequently bound up with their ambitious professional interests. If number nine people live a spiritual life, they are generally selfless, helpful, compassionate, agreeable, and charitable. Being full of energy and independent, nines strive to do and achieve great things, putting all their efforts into the cause of advancing humankind.

White labradorite (rainbow moonstone)* helps us to find inner balance. It reinforces our empathy and awakens our intuition. This gemstone shows us that life can be a game. It stimulates openness, spiritual breadth, and a zest for life. It also promotes calm and relaxation and brings about certain chance occurrences in order to make life enjoyable.

Charoite is a special healing crystal in times of change. It brings the gifts of great strength, courage, and persistence, and helps us to make important decisions. It reinforces our self-awareness and self-perception and boosts our aura system. People who wear it can accomplish great quantities of work thanks to its energy.

* White labradorite is mainly available as a gemstone, but occasionally also as a tumbled stone.

Weaknesses

Number nine people are sometimes wasteful and can be hungry for money and power. They are also said to be self-interested, irritable, impulsive, and intolerant, with blinkered attitudes. Nines have often had to contend with a wide range of problems—mainly within their family—during their childhood or youth, and as a result they can often be emotional, sensitive, and moody in their reactions to external influences; this is why they go out of their way to avoid conflict. They have a tendency to erupt in fits of rage, and to be thoughtless and tactless.

Hungry for knowledge and skills, number nines often want to do more than is possible, and so routinely feel they have bitten off more than they can chew. They like to do everything immediately and as far as they are concerned their many different plans should all have been carried out "the day before yesterday." They find it very difficult to make decisions as they don't like to be tied down; they are hesitant and yet impatient. Nines can be egocentric dreamers, characterized by both compassion and self-pity; they have a fear of commitment and yet want to be pampered. Number nine people should finish one venture before starting on another, in both their private and professional lives. They will achieve success in adulthood, by which time they should have learned to put away their self-doubt and master self-control.

Noble serpentine brings a sense of calm to those who wear it, allowing them to pause to take a breath and in the silence, perceive a presence that is divine. It has a relaxing effect on the body, balances out stress blockages, and alleviates mood swings.

Kunzite achieves very good results when used for mental suffering caused by emotional issues. It helps us to overcome inner resistance, strengthens the nerves when we are under great strain, and provides a metaphorical shoulder to lean on during relationship problems. Its liberating effect makes us more open-minded and upbeat.

Peridot exerts a strong influence on the moods of those who wear it. It mitigates external influences and burdens, while easing feelings of self-reproach and guilt; it helps us to admit to and forgive our own mistakes. It makes us sociable and tolerant, helping us to bring previous chapters in our lives to a close and opening our eyes to new beginnings.

Ambitions

Number nine people have an unconditional love for humanity and all creation. Their goal is to follow their own individual path to mastery with tolerance and to complete the transformation from an ego-based personality to that of a master.

Selflessness and empathy are crucial for nines. Thanks to their wealth of experience from the challenges and changes that they undergo in life, they can share the knowledge they have acquired along the way. They should follow their intuition, act to put their dreams into practice, and make use of their psychic abilities for the good of everyone. For number nines, true happiness is to be found in serving others. When they open their generous hearts, they can enfold everyone with their love. Number nine people will then no longer be satisfied with what is on the outside in life but will want to get inside themselves and understand why everything is the way it is; they want to perceive things as they truly are, letting go of everything and living in the "here and now."

Crystals that support ambitions

Smoky quartz brings the highest light powers to this earthly plane and helps us when we are striving for spiritual realization and trying to strip away the material things that hold us down. This gemstone relaxes fixed mental attitudes and patterns of thinking and is very effective against stress, tension, and depressive moods. It is often used when a great trauma or misfortune has occurred; it also helps people who find it difficult to accept certain inevitabilities in life and thus have a tendency to want to escape or look for a way out. It is excellent for helping to deal with all kinds of addiction, providing particular support for "smoke"-ers.

Orthoclase helps in the transition to new consciousness. It "shakes us awake" to prepare for inner change and to let go of fear of failure and self-centeredness.

Affirmations

- I am opening myself up to new things and a higher plane, and I trust my dreams and visions.
- I allow my heart to be my guide, follow my intuition, and use my psychic abilities for the good of all.
- I live in the present, I am centered, I look after myself, and I shape my path in accordance with my life purpose.

Other balancing and harmonizing crystals

Honey calcite activates our powers of self-healing. It radiates great warmth and helps us to accept life in a positive manner, providing the best conditions for our work and our life circumstances.

Lepidolite helps us to experience new developments calmly and without fanfare. It protects against external influences, and reduces stress, fears, and gloomy feelings. It enables us to concentrate on what is essential and to make confident decisions.

Number 9 shows us that we are whole and healthy when Heaven and Earth are united within us. With it we can recognize that there are no irreconcilable opposites and that instead they permeate and enrich one another.

Healing effects on the body

Red jasper stimulates the blood circulation and the metabolism. It can be used against all kinds of inflammation, as well as for all ear, nose, and throat complaints, rheumatism, and heart problems. It strengthens the joints and the entire skeleton, and sharpens our senses of taste and smell.

White labradorite regulates the female hormonal cycle and boosts our body awareness.

Charoite is a powerful crystal against pain; it also reinforces the immune system and calms the nerves.

Noble serpentine helps against asthma and kidney problems; it is good at removing toxins and soothes heartburn.

Kunzite reinforces the organic function of the heart, regulates thyroid function, and helps to ease neuralgia and toothache.

Peridot stimulates the liver and gall bladder, removes toxins, harmonizes the metabolism, and is good against warts, diabetes, and weakness of the connective tissue.

Smoky quartz exerts a calming influence and is analgesic (for the back); it can be used against radiation exposure and firms up connective tissue and muscles.

Orthoclase improves vision as we get older, helps with heart conditions, and harmonizes hormonal production.

Honey calcite restores youthfulness and reinforces bones, teeth, and connective tissue.

Lepidolite helps to combat complaints involving sciatica and neuralgia, alleviates itching and psoriasis, and promotes restful sleep.

The Number 0

We all have big changes in our lives that are more or less a second chance.

HARRISON FORD (AMERICAN ACTOR)

The American mathematician Robert Kaplan once said: "If you look at zero you see nothing; but look through it and you will see the world."

Although zero (0) does not play a part in name analysis, it is nonetheless extremely important in numerical terms, which is why it is included here. Its position in a number is significant (01, 10, 100, ... for example); it represents change and prepares us for a higher plane. Zero helps us to attain the next level—added to 1, it becomes 10. Number 0 teaches us to look ahead and cast off any doubts we have about our lives.

When calculating our numbers, the result is 0 when an expression number or date of birth contains 19, 28, 37, or 46....; when these numbers are added together, the total is 10.

In addition, for someone born in the tenth month or with a birthday on the 10th, 20th, or 30th day of the month, the 0 indicates new possibilities. The year of birth number is similarly important (for example, 1990, 2010, 2020....).

The key to 0 is trust; then resolution and liberation can take place for the benefit of everyone. The 0 unites archetypes (the numbers 1–9) to form a whole.

Symbolism

Although 0 is still a relatively young number, first used around 1,000 years ago, its symbol, a circle, is one of the most ancient signs used by humankind. It represents perfection, the female principle, the roundness of the Earth, harmony, wholeness, and unity. The ellipse (an oval) is also used to represent 0 and conveys a sense of safety and protection, like the aura that cocoons the body. It is the primal form of all planetary frequencies.

The transformed **Pluto** is an important planet for 0; Pluto governs the zodiac sign of Scorpio and is the higher octave of the planet Mars. Transformed, Pluto symbolizes the magical aspect of our personality, the side of us that is aware of the power of our imagination and the energetic fundamentals of life, and is confident in its own power and creative strength.

The power of the planet **Uranus** also forms part of 0's energy. Once Uranus has been released within us, powerful energies will come to the fore. Autonomy, personal responsibility, and shared ideals will become part of life; we can leave behind restrictive structures and old ways of thinking and behaving. Zero's strong, positive power can then be put to use.

When a number is placed in front of 0, its meaning is increased tenfold, a hundredfold, and so on. Every number can therefore be multiplied to infinity.

The 0 is the absolute expression of God's boundless creative potential.

Sugilite is very special, uniting within it all that is heavenly and all that is earthly. It has been described as a "New Age" stone as it boosts consciousness and stabilizes the psyche. Sugilite helps us to be open to change and therefore provides support when we are fearful and are undergoing difficult life situations. It brings the gifts of wisdom, clarity, and boundless energy.

Talents and Abilities

Zero is the number of transformation and new beginnings. We connect with it to unite our souls with the Divine. Zero represents power and energy that is not yet present but may yet still come about. It closes the circle of numbers and combines the powers of number 9 to form a whole, bringing humankind into a new cycle of tens.

For zero people, life has any number of challenges, with constant change and transformation. Despite external adversity, they are able to express their own individuality and as travelers between worlds they are always in the right place at the right time. Zero people also look ahead to the future and so are often one step ahead of others. However, they do not forget to live in the present. Their particularly powerful intuition allows them to dare to innovate.

Zero people strive for wisdom and so demonstrate potential for great spiritual growth. Blessed with good memories and powerful imaginations, they have the ability to think on a grand scale, seeing the big picture. They also favor a gentle approach, acting in a conciliatory and consolidating manner. They are caring, reliable, and flexible, believing in the essential good in others. Zero people feel they are part of a greater whole, and everyone is equal in their eyes. They therefore interact with others in a friendly, open, and helpful manner, with no ulterior motive; instead their focus is on openness, being non-judgmental, fair, and objective.

Crystals that boost talents and abilities

Watermelon tourmaline is one of the most diverse gemstones in the mineral kingdom. It channels and guides our energy, both physical and mental, and so connects every aspect of our being—our life experiences, opinions, and attitudes are all brought together in a meaningful context. It also enhances the body's vibrations, boosts spiritual activity, and fosters openness and tolerance. Every day is a new beginning and has something special in store for the soul; it demonstrates the diversity of what is possible.

Larimar brings happiness and exerts a protective effect. It aligns with human consciousness and is an excellent crystal for light-work and healing. It reminds people of their "higher selves" and, if it is in harmony with our soul's destiny, will give us what we long for. It brings inner peace, reveals creative solutions, rewards honesty, reinforces self-discipline, increases sensitivity, and helps the mind to simply allow things to happen, rather than trying to manipulate proceedings.

Zero people like to get to straight the point and so often blurt things out without thinking. They don't like taking orders—if you try to convince them to do something, you can be sure they will do the opposite. They are extremely stubborn, selfish, clingy, and restless, with a tendency to be oversensitive. If they don't keep their eccentricity and obstinacy in check, they risk appearing rebellious, although in fact this is the last thing they would want. Sometimes it is almost as though they have a death wish, risking their lives when they push their limits in taking on hazardous challenges. Their thinking can be hopelessly confused, but they are happy to sacrifice themselves for others, either because they are seeking recognition or are scared of being chastised.

Crystals that balance out weaknesses

Stromatolite makes life enjoyable and varied, with periods of rest, relaxation, and activity. It makes us willing to compromise so that we can go with the flow of life. This makes it an ideal meditation crystal as it helps us to process our experiences in life.

Blue quartz has a gentle effect on the wearer and is quick to help soothe racing thoughts. It conveys calm and patience, and promotes empathy; it combats discontent and self-loathing, and cleanses our minds and our moods. This gemstone also instills stability and has a reenergizing effect.

Aragonite brings a sense of calm to the oversensitive and those who feel restless or uneasy, or to those who tend to act rashly and in a volatile manner. It has a stabilizing effect on spiritual development and is good at preserving calm in stressful situations. Thanks to its capacity for promoting concentration, it is useful in situations where we need to be silent and still.

Pyrite sun* brings light and has a stimulating effect on all our chakras. It stabilizes mind and body and brings about great change in life. It is particularly useful against self-loathing or even a death wish, as it infuses the body with love.

Ambitions

Zero people want to understand others and bring them together as a community. Their goal is to find masterful perfection in their own individuality in order to prepare their fellow human beings for a new world and to lead them there. New opportunities and ways forward will present themselves and if zero people face up to their challenges, they will find realistic solutions to their problems. Their ability to get through life—plowing a solitary furrow if they have to—gives zero people the courage to complete new and even quite unconventional projects, supported by their good memories and powerful imaginations. They get along well with other people and prove sociable companions and

* Pyrite sun is available only as a disk-shaped mineral or as smaller fragments of this.

skillful speakers. Their big concern is to "act for the good of all while harming no one."

Crystals that support ambitions

Agates** bring good luck for the new era, along with inner stability and spiritual maturity, protection and a sense of security. They also instill courage and persistence.

Peace agate deserves special mention in relation to the zero. It helps peace to come to the world, while its white light dispels violence and aggression. It promotes purity, insight, and patience, and provides support in the conscious processing of our experiences. Agates that contain clear quartz at their core boost our powers of recall, even of the time before birth and/or after death.

---

* The agate family is varied with a particularly wide range of signature styles. The best known are Botswana agate, lace agate, fire and water agate, snakeskin, peace, and dendritic agate.

Affirmations

- All possibilities and new paths are opening within me. Joy, strength, and courage are my companions.
- My intuitions and perceptions are strong; I have unlimited potential at my disposal and I trust my universal guidance.
- I perfectly inhabit the "here and now," and I use my abilities for the good of all.

Other balancing and harmonizing crystals

Beige-brown "cappuccino" jasper centers us, bringing calm, persistence, and grounding. It is perfect for gentle, diffident people as it instills strength, expressive power, and commitment; it also promotes maturity and stability.

Vesuvianite helps us to assimilate all aspects of our personalities and helps to free us from addiction and bad habits. It grounds us in the real world and makes us strong and consistent.

Chrysopal opens us up to new sensations and experiences, encourages our sense of community, brings enthusiasm, and stimulates child-like curiosity. It also helps if we are in need of emotional release and will take the weight of the world from our shoulders, allowing us to see the miracles of life.

Healing effects on the body

Sugilite can be used in cancer therapy and for mental health problems. As it alleviates pain, it has a powerful effect on physical illnesses.

Watermelon tourmaline promotes the regeneration of nerves, is effective against multiple sclerosis, and helps couples trying to start a family.

Larimar eases birth trauma and promotes growth in children; it reinforces bone and has a positive effect on the airways.

Stromatolite is useful against intestinal disorders. It also helps to boost the metabolism and encourages mobility.

Blue quartz calms the nerves and alleviates pain in chronic back strain.

Aragonite regenerates intervertebral discs and helps combat meniscus and joint pain.

Pyrite sun is effective against all kinds of pain, sciatica, and rheumatism, and helps to soothe knee and back complaints; it also provides support against diabetes.

Agate is good for mother and child during pregnancy and helps with conditions affecting the skin and womb; it also reduces inflammation in the stomach area.

Beige-brown "cappuccino" jasper can be used for the stomach and colon.

Vesuvianite detoxifies and deacidifies the body.

Chrysopal detoxifies and strengthens the kidneys and the immune system. It also helps to ease water retention.

Meditation with Numbers and Healing Crystals

The **numbers** that we calculate in numerology reveal the strengths and weaknesses in our personalities that are expressed in our lives.

The vibrations of healing **crystals** can stimulate spiritual growth and promote our personal development.

Think about the numbers that you have calculated and decide which is of particular importance to you at the moment, along with a topic or issue that you wish to concentrate on. Now choose a suitable crystal.

Find a calm and peaceful place in your home or perhaps outside among nature. Begin by cleansing and releasing any troublesome emotions to prepare yourself for a meditative state of mind; breathe in and out calmly and be aware of the way the muscles in your body are relaxing.

Place your chosen crystal on your solar plexus, visualize your favorite number or your number code, and imagine this/these number(s) touching your aura a thousand times with divine, silvery light. Imagine yourself breathing in this healing light and these number vibrations as they spread throughout your whole body.

Enjoy this moment; sense how it is filled with joy, love, and peace. Your crystal is now similarly infused with this positive energy and will be with you throughout the day.

If you would like to work with several crystals together, I recommend the following:

Inside a crystal circle

Choose three crystals each from among the crystals recommended for your expression, destiny, and realization numbers (making a total of nine power crystals).

- Find a quiet place in your home, or perhaps outside among nature.
- Arrange your selected crystals in a circle. It is best to keep the main crystal—the most important crystal—in your left hand (or place it on your heart chakra).
- Sit or lie down in the center of the circle and get comfortable.
- As crystals "radiate" a presence, make sure you feel at ease in the crystal circle. If you feel any anxiety or a little hemmed in, make the circle a little bigger. Once you are feeling relaxed and calm, make contact with "your" healing crystal, the one that you feel most connected with intuitively or that represents the most important issue for you currently.
- Connect with Mother Earth and activate your energy system (with its seven chakras), so that you can perceive the higher planes of light. Your crown chakra is open and you are centered on your heart.

- Let go of your old beliefs and entrenched attitudes. Breathe in and out calmly. Your body is completely relaxed; live solely in the moment.
- Absorb the vibration of the crystals you have selected. While in this meditative state, visualize your healing number code (made from your expression, realization, and life path numbers, see page 10–11); repeat the number softly to yourself, over and over, and allow the radiating power of the crystal circle to work its effect.
- Instead of the code, you might repeat one of the affirmations relating to your number. For example, "I perfectly express my divine light."
- Pay attention to your feelings, thoughts, and emotions.
- Take your time. Enjoy the silence and absorb the new, bright vibrations with your mind, body, and soul.
- Remain in your crystal circle until you have a clear sense that you should bring the meditation to an end. Now gently begin to move your arms, legs, and head, and return to the "here and now."
- How do you feel? Sense the positive energy that the crystals have transmitted to you, and feel how you are now filled with energy and yet are completely relaxed at the same time, ready to take on your day.
- After your meditation, spend some time reflecting upon your ideas and train of thought. Take note of the people you meet and what conversations or situations arise.

Crystal/number installation

This is another way in which crystals can help you:

- Draw a circle on a piece of card and and in the center write your name (first and last names, as used in your calculation) and your date of birth. Place your most important crystal, (the one that means the most to you) in the center of the circle, then arrange the remaining 8 crystals around it, placing them over the circle outline.

- Now place your arrangement in a quiet position in your home and leave it to do its work.

There are sure to be some healing crystals that you already trust and work with, but you may find activating certain others more of a challenge.

Have faith in your intuition and follow your gut feeling about which crystals you need and when. The crystals you have selected through your calculations (or intuitively) will reveal your abilities, but they may also reveal your limitations. You will undoubtedly discover traits of which you were previously unaware, as well as the potential you have to express aspects of your personality even more clearly. Work with crystals of good quality—slightly larger stones have a more intense effect than smaller ones. Choose crystals that appeal to you intuitively, those that seem to be saying "I am the right one."

Dear readers,

As I (Editha Wuest) have been working with gemstones, healing crystals, numerology, and alternative healing methods for years, and I love to advise people who come to me, I am delighted that I am now able to pass on my knowledge in this book. I have also had much support, suggestions, and encouragement from the spiritual world; so I would like to thank everyone from the bottom of my heart.

I (Sabine Schieferle) am also glad that I have once again been able to be part of this book project; knowledge has been refreshed, and many new things have been added. For me—as for you, the reader—a time of practical application is now beginning.

We wish our readers all the very best, with much new inspiration and acts of divine providence, so that you can follow your destined paths in love, strength, joy, and courage. Allow yourself to blossom in every way and aspect and recognize your own creative powers. May trust and patience be your companions as you follow your path.

With the greatest sincerity and solidarity,
Editha Wuest and Sabine Schieferle

Please feel free to contact Editha Wuest if you have any further questions: wuest.editha@gmx.de

Costelloe, Marina: *The Complete Guide to Manifesting with Crystals*, Earthdancer/Inner traditions, 2009

Crawford Saffi/Sullivan, Geraldine: *The Power of Attraction: The Astrological Guide to Personal Success, Prosperity, and Happy Relationships*, Ballantine Books, 2002

Gienger, Michael: *Crystal Power, Crystal Healing*, Cassell; new edition 2005

Gienger, Michael: *Healing Crystals: The A – Z Guide to 555 Gemstones*, revised edition, Earthdancer /Inner traditions, 2014

Neumayer, Petra, Stark, Roswitha: *Painting the Energy Body: Signs and Symbols for Vibrational Healing*, 2013

Parker, Steve: *Rocks and Minerals* (Eyewitness Explorers), DK Children, 1993

Index of Crystals

About the Authors

Editha Wuest has been working with crystals, numerology, and alternative healing methods for many years. Since 1995 she has maintained her own counselling and coaching practice and leads seminars and courses. She lives near Munich, Germany.

Sabine Schieferle is a numerologist with many years of experience. She lives near Munich, Germany.

Picture Credits

All crystal photographs are by Ines Blersch
Page 15: Von Gaak/shutterstock.com
Page 42, 88: Karola Sieber.

For further information and to request a book catalogue contact:
Inner Traditions, One Park Street, Rochester, Vermont 05767

Earthdancer Books is an Inner Traditions imprint.
Phone: +1-800-246-8648, customerservice@innertraditions.com
www.earthdancerbooks.com • www.innertraditions.com

EARTHDANCER

AN INNER TRADITIONS IMPRINT